The Writ

Guilty or Innocent,

You decide

By

R. Merial Martin

ISBN 978-1463597184

All Rights accrue to the author, R. Merial Martin

Printed in the United States of America

Author's Note

Out of respect for their privacy, I have changed the names of all of the people whose names appear in these pages.

FOREWORD

The writ of habeas corpus, usually used to test the legality of a prisoner's detention, has expressly been preserved because it is explicitly mentioned in the United States Constitution (thus, it probably cannot be abolished except by constitutional amendment). In the United States federal courts, the writ is most often used to review the constitutionality of criminal convictions rendered by state courts.

By statute, the Supreme Court of the United States uses the writ of certiorari to review cases from the United States courts of appeals or from the state courts.

In extraordinary circumstances, the United States court of appeals can use the common-law writ of prohibition under the All Writs Act to control proceedings in the district courts.

Some courts have held that in rare circumstances in a federal criminal case, a United States district court may use the common-law writ of error "coram nobis" under the All Writs Act to set aside a conviction when no other remedy is available.

The United States district courts normally follow state-court practice with respect to certain provisional remedies and procedures for enforcement of civil judgments, which may include writs of attachment and execution, among others.

Certain other writs are available in theory in the United States federal courts but are almost never used in practice. In modern times, the All Writs Act is most commonly used as authority for federal courts to issue injunctions to protect their jurisdiction or effectuate their judgments.

The situation in the courts of the various U.S. states varies from state to state but is often similar to that in the federal courts. Some states continue to use writ procedures, such as quo warranto, that have been abolished as a procedural matter in federal courts.

In an attempt to purge Latin from the language of the law, California law has for many years used the term *writ of mandate* in place of *writ of mandamus*, and *writ of review* in place of *writ of certiorari*. Early efforts to replace *writ of habeas corpus* with *writ of have the body* never caught on.

A Writ takes in all of the evidence of a trial, the appeals, and reviews defense and prosecutions representations to determine whether a petitioner was afforded a fair and impartial trial. It also searches to find inconsistencies in the defense, prosecution, and/or defense/prosecution collaborations that may have created ineffective counsel for the petitioner.

Introduction

Roger Jason Lee has been incarcerated since 1980. He has been refused parole on seven different occasions. In 2000 he was told that he would not be eligible to seek parole for seven years. He has maintained his innocence and because he has never admitted to attempted murder and expressed his regrets in a parole hearing, he remains in prison. His time in prison has been a model as he has learned skills that allow him to be certified as a Braille translator. He spends his days translating literary books and textbooks into Braille for the blind citizens of America.

He knows that if he gives in and states his guilt and remorse that he will have to spend even more time because, as the system works, the parole board would state that he was just trying to please them by saying what they want to hear, so he could be found suitable for parole. And also that he should have had remorse from the beginning resulting in the board needing more time to evaluate his sincerity. Had he been able to admit guilt pre-trial and get a plea bargain for eight years, he would have been out and, no doubt, building a good life for himself and his family.

A Writ was performed Attorney James Swank and his staff of investigators to be accepted by the courts. Roger's story is laid out herein and readers of his story and arrest have an opportunity to decide in a juror's, attorney's, or judge's shoes, the innocence or guilt in this Writ.

When reading the "True Writ", all references to precedent setting cases, trial evidence, and police document pages are (bracketed) to have all inclusive data remain intact. Readers may want to bypass the bracketed references and numbers and absorb only the statements. Legal experts reading this novel will understand and follow the path of the references.

THE CASE

The noise from the gas-powered steam cleaning machine spills throughout the fast food restaurant. It is 2 AM. The restaurant is closed for business and Roger and his co-worker, Chuck, are the only ones on site. Chuck is on the roof and has uncoupled the grill vents in order to have access to steam clean the grease out of the flue and into large trash cans that Roger has placed under the vent hoods."

"Okay Chuck, you can start spraying the cleaner now", yells Roger as he begins to spray upwards into the flue. They would let that spray chemical set for three minutes and then Chuck would snake the sprayer down from the roof through the vent to wash the greasy residue down into the trash cans under the vents.

"That's it Chuck. Shut it off. We do not want the trash cans to overflow. I believe we have got all the grease out of this flue and the vent. Uncouple the other one while I drain the can and scrape the grease out so it can be recycled."

"Gotcha", yells Chuck.

Roger hooks a hose to the next vent. Then he uses a shopvac to suck grease and water from the hood and floor. He wraps the next hood in plastic and places the trash cans underneath the hood.

They completed the job and while gathering up the steam machine and all their equipment, Chuck notices a set of keys on the sales counter.

"Look Roger, I guess the night manager forgot his keys".

Roger told Chuck to just leave them where they are.

"The morning gal will find them when she opens. We still have our door key to lockup as we leave."

This was the one night, however, that a manager would not be there to turn on the alarm when the steam cleaners left the building. Many times the night manager would stay until the crew was finished cleaning the vents and then alarm and lock the building. This manager, however, would usually tell the crew that he was leaving and to lock the door with their key. Chuck thinks, *Maybe he left the keys so the cleaning crew could set the alarm.*

"Yeah, Roger, it looks like there are office and safe keys. That manager is irresponsible.

"Okay, Chuck, just like I said, leave them there, the morning gal will find them, and she may report it to the owner."

Chuck and Roger are outside near their trucks. They both drive their own vehicles because of the equipment they must carry. Sometimes they also do a one-man cleaning job. They talk about the jobs they have to do in the San Fernando Valley tomorrow night.

"So long, Chuck. Get some sleep. The job in the Valley is a big one. That new Burger King really greases up the vents. We may need two vat pans for each vent."

Roger drives to his apartment where his wife, Mary and her sister, Paula live. Paula shares the two bedroom apartment with them. The women are asleep, but Mary wakes when she hears Roger in the shower. Mary is pregnant with their first child.

"Honey, I can't sleep, I need something to eat. Will you take me to breakfast?"

"Sure, Mary, but it is 4 AM!"

"I know, but you know my condition and I know you want to please me."

Roger takes Mary to a 24-hour Burger King and orders from the drive-thru window. They return home, but Mary has finished her order before Roger turns into the driveway. He hands his order over to her and smiles.

THE PRIOR

Roger had a humble beginning and a life with some stress and trauma due to the passing of his father, but he made the adjustment much better his siblings when his mother remarried. He grew up with good principles and was involved in his family church. Life in Los Angeles was filled with lots of friends but two which his step-father, Charles warned him about because he tended to allow them to lead him in their ways rather than he become the peer model for them to follow. One of his friends, Billy, was into gang activity and owned a car which Roger really wanted. He was going to high School and working part time at a fast food restaurant. Unknowing to his father, Charles, and his mother, Barbara, he had been paying Billy towards purchasing the car. His girlfriend was Eve. She was Caucasian and he was Black. She was promiscuous and flaunted herself on Roger. He was naïve and taken in by her. Roger spent his paycheck on Eve and the car payments to Billy. Eve would ask him for things and he saved up and got them for her. He was hooked. It was during that week when his parents went on vacation that they allowed Roger to stay home alone. He would visit their friends, the Smiths, across the street for dinner, go to school, and work while they were gone.

Eve pressured Roger into buying her a ring and Billy had given him an ultimatum to finish paying off the car or Roger might lose all that he had paid Billy. He decided to get the money by robbing his place of work. He removed the screen from the ceiling in the women restroom and climbed into the attic. He stayed there until the manager had closed up for the night. He climbed down and went to the cash drawers and emptied them netting over eight hundred dollars. He climbed back into the attic and stayed until the restaurant had opened that Saturday morning and he was to report for work. He made his way to the Men's restroom, cleaned up his face, and combed his hair. He wore a large afro during those times. The day manager was in his office talking to the police. Others employees greeted Roger and told him about the missing money but there was no apparent break in. Roger joined in with the employees and began preparing for their workday. The day manager felt that the night manager was involved. The owner was on his way down and had called the night manager to meet him at the business. Neither Roger nor the other employees were suspects. The owner fired the night manager because he could not prove that he had followed the weekend procedure by placing more change money in the cash boxes for the weekend and locking up the building.

Roger got the ring for Eve the next day and paid Billy more money to get him to agree to wait on the balance. Billy was happy and let Roger drive the car but he had to return it before his parents came back from vacation on the next Tuesday.

He felt that he had gotten away with the theft. He was quieter than normal when he greeted his parents on their return. The Smiths across the street had nothing but glowing remarks for the way Roger had handled himself with them and for going to school and work and not having anyone in the house. At least what they could see from the front. However, Roger had let Eve into the house from the rear door. His parents would learn that later.

Summertime came and Roger began working fulltime and was making more money. He was spending more on Eve than he was paying Billy for the car. He still had not told his parents about the car. The Fourth of July weekend was here and Roger knew there would be lots of cash in the cash boxes for change. Things had been quiet at work and no longer was anyone talking about the theft of a couple of months ago.

Roger climbed back into the attic that Thursday night. The lights were turned off inside the building and he thought he heard the manager lock the door and leave. He climbed down into the Ladies restroom and heard a noise. Someone was still in the building. He donned a ski mask and decided that if the manager was still there he would make him open the safe. He could get to the kitchen and grab a weapon, a knife, and force the manager to open the safe. On the way to the manager's office in the back of the building he opened the cash drawers and put all the bills into his jacket pockets. The manger had heard a noise and ran to the counter area with mace in hand. Before Roger knew he was there, he felt the burning spray of the mace and began wilding swinging the large kitchen knife. He cut the manager on the left arm and then on the right. There was dim lighting and neither of them could be seen clearly, but the manager knew it was an employee because of the uniform pants and he recognized that employee to be Roger because of his build that was not like any other male employee. The manager went to the floor screaming and that caused Roger to bolt out of the kitchen, open the door, and run all the way to his home. His parents were asleep and he went into the bathroom and tried to wash the mace from his face and eyes. He could not get rid of the smell and went into his bedroom on the opposite end of the house from the other three bedrooms.

Charles Lee was fast asleep when the doorbell rang. He grabbed a robe, donned it, and walked steadfastly towards the front door. He peered through the peephole and could see the two police officers on the front porch shining a flashlight upwards towards their chins.

"Who is it?" Charles asked.

"We are from the LAPD", one of the replied.

"What do you need?" asked Charles.

"We want to talk to Roger Lee. Are you Roger Lee?" the officer in front asked.

"No, Roger is my son". Still speaking through the closed door, "What do you want to talk to him about?

"There was a robbery at his workplace and we need to ask him some questions."

Charles Lee thought for a few seconds before responding. He was sure that Roger should be in bed. Charles opened the front door. A screen door was still latched. The officer in front pulled on it only to learn that it was latched.

"I will go and get Roger to see if he can help you." "Where is Roger?" asked the lead officer.

"He should be asleep in his room", replied Charles.

"Can we go with you?" asked the second officer.

"No, but you can come into the living room and wait while I bring him to you." Charles said as he unlocked the screened door. Both officers stepped inside, flashlights still on. Charles started walking through the den towards the kitchen where Roger's room was off the utility room. He opened the door to Roger's room and to his surprise the two officers moved pass him and went to Roger's bedside. They could see both his hands and while shinning the light into his face, they could see the scarring from the mace attack.

"Roger, I need you to slowly get out of bed and standup", demanded the lead officer. "Wow, can you smell that mace? It is very strong in this room", announced the second officer.

Charles was speechless and then asked, "Why didn't you wait for me to bring him to you? What is that smell?"

The lead officer was busy handcuffing Roger and stated, "Mr. Lee, Roger is a suspect in the robbery at the restaurant and we need to talk to him. We will take him back to the restaurant to try to clear up this matter."

"Roger, what happened to your face, son?" asked Charles.

Roger did not speak to his father as the officers lead him through the house towards the front door. Roger still had his work pants and a T-shirt on. The second officer lead Roger to the patrol car parked in the driveway. The lead officer stopped at the front door and told Charles that Roger had been identified as the robber, and had cut the night manager on the arms with a kitchen knife. That it was the manager who sprayed him in the face with mace. That was why the room smelled of mace and Roger's face was scarred.

"So how is the manager?" asked Charles.

"He is okay, the paramedics bandaged him, and he is waiting there for us before he goes to the emergency room for treatment. Mr. Lee, we will return in about thirty minutes and hopefully have more information to clear this up."

The officers got into the patrol car, backed out of the driveway, and headed in the direction the fast food place.

Barbara and the other children were still fast asleep. How would he explain that Roger may have committed a crime and injured someone? This was so difficult to accept because of all their teachings, their church involvement, the boy scouts, organized football, and baseball that Roger was a party to and whose training and guidance should have never led him into crime. He walked into the master bedroom and asked Barbara to get up and come with him. He sat down on the couch and she next to him. He told her of everything that happened from the time he answered the door to when the patrol car drove off with Roger handcuffed in the rear seat. While telling her, Barbara's eyes filled with tears from the first words about the police entering the house without a warrant and not even asking if Charles agreed to them going into Roger's room. She could not believe that Roger could have been involved in such a crime.

They walked into Roger's room.

"Is that the smell you talked about", she asks.

"Yes, the police knew it right away."

"I just do not understand how he could do anything like that. And why? He did not need money. We always gave him what he needed, and, he had money from his job. I bet it was because of that girl. I am sure she caused him to try and do this for money for her."

"I tend to believe you are right, Barbara. I will bet you that she was the reason. Just look at his room. Everything is neat. He is not like most teenagers we know whose parents complain about how sloppy they are."

The doorbell rings.

"Oh! The police must be back."

They walk through the kitchen and into the living room. Opening the front door, they see the lead Policeman. The other is in the car with Roger. Charles opens the screened door and lets the officer into the living room.

"You folks might want to sit down and I'll tell you what has happened."

They all move to the couch. The Lees sit down and the officer is standing in front of them.

"Roger admitted to the crime. Now although he did not intend to hurt anyone, he says that when the mace was sprayed into his eyes that he reacted by wildly swinging the knife. He says he did not know that he had cut the manager until he heard him scream and go to the floor. That is when he ran out of the building and came straight to his house. He says that he hid the money in the backyard under a bush. We need to retrieve it and hold it for evidence. The manager was taken to the emergency room for treatment. He will be okay. There is no deep, life threatening wounds. We stopped by to tell you that we have arrested Roger and we are taking him to the station for booking. The manager did say that Roger was a great kid and he would have never expected him to do this. Somebody or something caused him to change. I hope it was not drugs. Well that is all I have to say at this point. Do either of you have questions for me?"

Charles asks, "Can we talk to Roger? Can you bring him into the house?"

"First, I need you to walk with me to the backyard to look for the money. Then I will see what I can do. I will have to call my sergeant to get clearance."

Charles takes the officer into the backyard. They go to the only bush near the gate and there was a paper bag. The officer picked it up and opened it. He showed the money to Charles and they walked back into the house.

The officer walked out to the car and handed the bag to his partner who is sitting in the front seat. He sits on the driver's side and calls into his duty sergeant.

"You got the money, the knife, and the guy in custody, so bring him in right now. His parents can see him after he is booked", the sergeant's voice could be overheard by the Lees who were standing on the front porch, still in their night clothing.

The sun had come up and neighbors had begun driving to work. Some slowed down to see what was going on and who was in the backseat of the police car.

"I think you could hear my sergeant's response. Here is the number and address of the station", as he hands Charles a card. "You folks can call after noontime and find out when you can see him."

The officer walks back to the car. He gets in and backs it out of the driveway. The Lees wave in Roger's direction as the police car speeds away. They hold each other closely and walk into the kitchen where Barbara starts to make coffee and toast. They are quiet for a few moments and gazing at the ceiling and towards Roger's bedroom door. They are both pondering how this could happen to their family. They felt they had always done all the right things to insure that their children would never lean towards crime as a means to an end. They did not deserve this. They had to talk to Roger to find out what caused him to do this. Why did he admit to it so fast? Was it because he had been sprayed with mace and it showed to his father and the police? Was it because he knew he had hurt the manager and that was something way beyond his desires when he decided to rob his workplace, again? Alternatively, was it because he knew that his parents had done the best they could in raising him to be a Christian and responsible young man, and he was sorry that he had hurt them? Charles and Barbara were leaning towards the latter conviction. As they sipped on coffee and ate toast, they talked about how they would tell family members, neighbors, friends, and more importantly, his siblings.

Charles called the police station around noon and learned they could visit Roger between 3 pm and 4pm. Barbara would stay home from work and keep the kids home from school. Charles had called in to work to take a vacation day. He had never been inside a police station. This was a frightening experience for him. Having seen many movies and television shows he thought it would look familiar to him, however this was different, and a real life change because his son was involved in a crime? He had to wait for nearly an hour before an officer took him to visit with Roger. As he sat on a bench he saw others who were arrested being brought into the station and led into rooms down the hallway. All he could think about was what his family and friends think of him and not what they would think about Roger. He felt that he had guilt for what his son had done. He was to blame for Roger's transgressions into crime.

Seated across from Roger, still handcuffed, but seated on the edge of a chair, making it even more difficult to fathom why they were both there, Charles asked Roger, why.

Roger hesitated and then said, "I don't know". "What do you mean, you don't know. You admitted to the police that you did it, told them where the money was hidden, brought this shame into our home and now you say you don't know why you did it?" " Come on, son." It was as if the use of the word, son, took on a different meaning to Roger. It meant that his father still considered him as his son. He was not talking down to him. He was just showing a heap of concern for his son.

"I needed the money, dad." "What did you need money for? Haven't we always given you everything you needed? Especially, when you were working part-time? What did you need money for?"

Their voices were not raised because there was an officer seated in the corner of the fifteen by twenty room. They spoke so that only they could hear what was being said. Charles was on one side of a desk and Roger on the other. They were both leaning over the desk, which was easy for Charles, but not so for Roger because of the handcuffing.

"I have been buying a car from Billy who lives around the corner from us. I have been paying him a little bit at a time until I could afford to pay all of it. I wanted to finally give him the money and get the car so I could surprise you 'all and show you I could do this on my own. I wanted to make you proud of me. Now I know I went about it the wrong way. Billy had been pressing me to pay him or he would keep the money I had paid him and keep the car. Now that will not happen. He will keep my money now because I will have to go to jail. Maybe you can go over and talk to his dad and get the money."

Charles looked at his son and thought to himself, *so that is why he did this.*

"Roger that was your second mistake. The first was to not talk to us about the car. The third was to think that you had to resort to crime in order to buy the car. What made you think you could get away with this? Haven't we taught you better? We are so hurt by what you have done. I am not concerned about the money you gave this kid. I just wished you had confided in us and not bring us to this disappointment. The detective told me that the manager thinks this is not your first time to take money from them. They had a theft a few months ago and it was the same "M.O." except for the assault to the manager. Do you have anything to say about that theft?"

Charles looked Roger square into the eyes. Roger cowered and looked down at the desk.

"I don't know anything about that time. This was the first time I tried something like this. I knew how someone was probably in the building and I figured that they had to use the ceiling in the restroom to hide until the business closed. What is going to happen to me, Dad? I am scared."

"Okay, I believe you. I will have to get you a lawyer, so do not talk about anything to the police until you talk to a lawyer. You are so naïve that you just told them all they need to know to get you convicted. You were not cut out to be a criminal. A criminal would not have come home knowing that he would get caught. A criminal would not have cooperated with the police. I know you are sorry for this mistake because of your actions with the police, but now is the time to keep everything to yourself. That way a judge may go easy on your sentence. I will take care of everything from here on out. I will see you again as soon as I can."

Charles stood up and the officer walked over and asked, "Are you done, Mr. Lee?" "Yes, I am and thank you."

Walking out of that room and leaving his son with the authorities was hard for Charles. Roger had not been away from home without family around at any time in his life. Of course he stayed at home alone when he and Barbara went on vacation, but the neighbors looked out for him. Here was a seventeen year old who had committed a crime of robbery and assault with a deadly weapon. That put him into manhood. He would have to pay for the crimes.

Charles called an attorney and asked him to look into Roger's case. A return phone call advised Charles to let Roger get a public defender. That because of his age, family background, and how contritely he gave up and gave information to the police, a judge would be lenient for his first offense. To hire him as an attorney would be a waste of money because he could do no more that a public defender would. Charles understood what the attorney was advising. The case on Roger went as he said and they judge sentenced him to one year in a juvenile facility. The one year came about because the manager who was cut by Roger wrote a letter to the judge praising Roger's work and saying that he did not understand why he did this, but did understand that Roger did not intend on cutting him. He knew that after he sprayed the mace that Roger became enraged and started swinging wildly. Roger served his time and came home. He was too old to go back to high school and started taking night classes.

While he was serving time, Charles and Barbara cleaned out his room and found receipts for $1200 for jewelry that coincided with the dates that they had been away on vacation which was right after the date that the business had been robbed. They knew that Roger had lied about the first robbery. This was his first crime. They knew that he had done this for his girlfriend, Eve, who stopped speaking to him once he was arrested. That relationship was over and all for the good, so they thought. Charles had also gone over to Billy's house to talk to his father about the money that Roger had given Billy for the car. Billy had sold the car to someone else and since Roger did not have any receipts for the payments, Billy's father bluntly stated that he did not intend on pressing his son to pay back the money. Charles did not seek resolution. He surmised that the father and son were alike. Billy was a gang member and into drugs. Both he and his father were arrested for selling drugs and both went to prison about three months after Charles had visited.

Charles bought Roger a used car and when he crashed it on the 405 freeway, late at night and could not explain why he rammed into a wall underneath a bridge overpass with no other vehicle being involved. Charles called his aunt in an old settled Los Angeles neighborhood and sent him to spend some time with her and her husband. For three years Roger lived with them while working on the job with Ernest Steam Cleaning Company. He bought himself a new truck and was doing so good when he met Mary, married, and moved into an apartment that they shared with Mary's sister, Paula Jordan. Life was good. Mary had become pregnant and they looked forward to the responsibilities of a big family. Mary worked at the Fox Hills Mall and they were saving money in preparation for the birth of their first child.

THE CRIME

Rita Daniels was in her forties. She was a slightly stout woman with Middle Eastern features. Rita had worked at MacDonalds for years. She moved up through the ranks to become a night manager. She worked late after closing some nights catching up on the paperwork so the morning manager could begin the day without having to do the previous day's record keeping. This night was not like other nights. Rita was still in the restaurant some two hours longer than she would normally stay at 3 am. She had placed her eyeglasses on the desk in the manager's office as she was winding up doing the bookwork. She heard a knock at one of the doors near the front of the building. She had left the lights on in the interior, but all exterior lights were off, including the brand signs. Her first thought was to not go up front because if it was a customer, they would just go away after realizing this was not a 24-hour restaurant. *However, why was she in there so late and why did she decide to go up front and answer the door?*

Walking through the full lit kitchen area, she navigated around the counter and towards the door where the knocking was still being heard. As she approached she saw a Black man holding a set of keys in his right hand.

"Yes, what do you want?"

"I got some keys."

Rita thinks that this person looks like one from the steam cleaners and the keys to the trap door on the roof had been missing since last month when the steam cleaners were there to clean the vents. She opens the door and asks for his name.

"Roggie." At least that is what sounded it like. She reached for the keys but he still held them high in the air. It was too high for her to reach them because of her shorter height.

"I got fired because of these keys."

Rita did not have her glasses on so she could not make out the ring of keys he was holding.

"Well then give me the keys and I will have the manager write a letter to get your job back."

At that point the man was inside the building. He put the set of keys into his pants pocket, pulled out a knife out of the same pocket and told her,

"I said I got fired and now I have come here to get my compensation."

Seeing the attacker's actions and the knife, Rita ran around the counter and into the kitchen. The attacker was right behind her and pointing the knife in her direction with his arm extended. Through the kitchen area she moved as swift as she could. If she could make it to her office and close the door it would lock automatically. The attacker was within three feet of her and when she entered the office and grabbed the door to shut it, he placed his left arm against the door and stepped into the office.

"Open the safe", he yelled as he pointed the knife closer to her face. Fearing what he would do, Rita opened the safe and watched as he took paper money from the safe and placed it into a white money bag that was sitting next to the safe. She was on her knees and he told her to move to where he was pointing towards the back wall of the office.

44

"Turn off the light switch", as he pointed again to the wall. She turned off the light which darkened the office but there was still light coming in from the open door. The robber moved towards Rita. He swung the knife and cut her on the throat. He began wildly swinging the knife in her direction cutting her on the back and head. He began stabbing moves to her body as she moved on the floor in an attempt to get away from him. He stepped over her body, placed a knee onto her back, and tried to stab her in the head, but she saw it coming and swung her arm, causing his arm to move to the right. The knife hit the concrete floor and two-thirds of the blade of the small knife broke off. The attacker continued to try and stab her with the broken knife. She felt the blows of his hand more than the damaged knife. Then he stopped.

Crying out, Rita pleaded, "Why don't you just go. I'm going to bleed to death, so just go."

The robber backed away from her, clutching money bag, pulled the phone cord from the wall, snapping it in half. Standing in the office doorway he told her,

"You wait thirty minutes, because I will be watching the building."

Then he ran out of the building and got into a vehicle which Rita could hear an engine start. She struggled to stand but made it. The neck wound was not deep enough to cause her to lose too much blood. Fearing she might not be able to get help, she cleaned her glasses, put them on, and wrote a note. Rita walked through the kitchen area, holding onto the tables and then out of the building towards a 24-hour radio station.

Banging on the door, an employee could see that she was

bleeding, opened the door, and called 9-1-1.

THE ALIBI

Roger, his wife and sister-in-law were watching television that night until about midnight when he and Mary went to bed. It is possible that Roger got up around 1 AM and drove his truck to South Bay where he had a job to do. It is possible that when he arrived the restaurant was closed and there was no one to let him in or to unlock the entrance to the vents on the roof. He was too late to meet the night manager. He drove back towards home. The fuel warning light buzzed so he pulled into the first gas station that he found. He did make it back home and his wife woke up when she heard him come into the room.

"Roger, I am hungry again. Can you take me out to get breakfast?"

Hearing her, he responded and told her that it would be just a minute. They would wake her sister and ask if she wanted to go for breakfast with them. She just rolled over, kept quiet indicating she was not interested.

About nine o'clock that morning Roger went to work at Ernst Steam Cleaning. He was sitting at a table when around 11 AM; Detective Ford came in with his boss, Joe Ernst, and a uniformed police officer.

"Roger Lee?" he called.

"Yes", Roger replied.

"Please stand up from the table." Roger stood up and the uniformed cop took his arms and handcuffed them behind him.

"Why are you doing this?" Roger asked.

"You know the MacDonalds that you cleaned last month and the keys were missing, well it was robbed last night and the manager was almost killed. Well she said it was you who did it", Detective Ford informed.

Roger could see where this was going. He decided to not say that he had gone out on a job because he had gotten there late and his boss was standing there. Joe Ernst would certainly fire him for not doing that job. So immediately, he decided to say that he was home.

"Not me." It was not me. I was at home all night. You can ask my wife and her sister. We watched TV and then went to bed. My wife asked me to take her to breakfast around 4 AM and we went to Denny's. You can check with Denny's because I ordered a fast breakfast and I did not have to pay because they did not bring it in ten minutes."

"We will check that out, but since this dying woman named you, we have to take you in for questioning." Detective Ford and the officer patted Roger down, opened his fanny pack, and found a roll of bills and some other loose change. Then they walked him outside and searched his truck.

"You said 'dying woman'. Is she dead?" asked Roger. "No, she will recover from her injuries, but she thought she was going to die and wrote a note, saying that 'Roggie from the cleaning company did this'."

"Roggie, who is Roggie? My name is Roger."

"Close enough", the detective came back as he continued to look through Roger's truck. Finding nothing that could be determined as evidence, Detective Ford locked the truck and placed the keys into the fanny pack. They put Roger into the police car and the police

51

man drove away. Detective Ford stood there talking to Joe Ernst to get Roger's address and asking for any information that could tie Roger to the robbery and attempted murder.

"I need to go to his apartment to try and verify his alibi", stated Ford to Joe Ernst. "Thanks for all your help."

Ford drove to the address given him by Ernst. Knocking on the door, it opened almost at the same time. Paula Jordan was leaving the apartment to run an errand.

"Oh! You scared me." She said to Detective Ford.

"I am Detective Ford with the LAPD, is Mrs. Lee here?" he said while pointing to his badge attached to his belt.

"She is at work and what do you want with her?"

"Are you the sister?"

"Yes."

"Well I need to talk to you too. What is your name?"

"Why do you want to talk to me? My name is Paula Jordan."

"Can I come in so we can talk?"

"No, I don't think so. There is no one else here. We can talk right here."

Paula stepped out of the doorway to the steps.

"We have arrested your brother-in-law, Roger Lee. I need to ask you some questions about last night."

"Arrested Roger? What for?" She had a surprised look on her face.

"He has been accused of a robbery. Tell me what happened last night. What he at the apartment?"

"We watched TV together and after the Late Show Roger and Mary went to their bedroom. Early in the morning they knocked on my door and asked me to go to breakfast. I did not talk to them, because I was still half asleep."

"So they went to the bedroom. Did Roger leave the apartment, at all?"

"Well, he talked about going to work while we were watching TV, but I was paying more attention to the show and did not catch everything that was said. However, after watching TV, I went into the shower and

I saw some lights flashing through the window. It could have been Roger, but I don't know for sure."

"Okay, thanks. Miss Jordan. I may need to talk to you again. Here is my card. You can call me if you remember something else."

Ford was walking away when Paula asked, "Where is Roger so I can call my sister and tell her?"

"He is at the downtown jail. It does not look good for him. He also tried to kill someone last night." Ford kept walking to his police cruiser.

Paula was in shock and went back into the apartment. She had to call Mary and tell her what had happened.

Detective Ford thought that Roger Lee's alibi was broken since his sister-in-law said he had talked about going to work and also saw what she thought might be his truck lights shine on her bedroom window. So, Ford headed his vehicle towards the hospital where Rita Daniels was being cared for.

THE LINEUP

Rita Daniels had just gotten out of surgery to repair a collapsed lung when Detective Ford arrived. She was in stable condition when she was taken there by EMS in the early morning hours. She was hooked up to test tubes and IVs and her hands were, visibly, shaking. After clearing it with the nurse on duty, he went into the recovery room.

She was still groggy from the anesthesia.

"Miss Daniels, I am Detective Ford with the LAPD. I don't want to take up too much time but I need to know if this is the person who did this to you."

He gives her two Polaroid pictures of Roger and she holds them in her hands, shaking something fierce. She does not have her glasses on. She knew it was a

Black man and she thought it was Roggie from the steam cleaners.

"Yes, it looks like the guy from the steam cleaners."

"Are you positive? Is this the man who did this to you?"

"I don't have my glasses, but it looks like the guy I know from the steam cleaners. What is his first name?"

"It is Roger."

"Yes that is his name, Roggie. Then it must be him."

"Thanks, Miss Daniels."

Detective Ford left the hospital to head back to the courthouse to seek a search warrant for Roger's apartment since they had found shoe prints with blood stains on the floor of the restaurant. He was able to obtain the warrant on the next morning and went to Roger's apartment where he and other officers performed a search, found some Reebok tennis shoes that looked like the tracks at the restaurant and collected some other items of interest.

THE TRIAL

The trial was held in February and March of 1981. Roger was sentenced to fourteen years to life for robbery and attempted murder on March 15, 1981. It was the note written by a victim who thought she might die that caused the jury to vote guilty. Because there were many mistakes by the police and the prosecution during the investigation and the trials, coupled with possible complicity on the part of the court appointed attorneys who rendered ineffective counseling to Roger, a Writ was ordered and paid for by Roger's parents after two attempts to have appeals on habeas corpus processed.

THE TRUE WRIT

The true Writ investigation is as follows:

IN THE SUPERIOR COURT OF THE STATE OF CALIFORNIA FOR LOS ANGELES COUNTY

In re ROGER JASON LEE,
Petitioner,

Los Angeles County Superior Court No.425005-Z

PETITION FOR WRIT OF HABEAS CORPUS

TO THE HONORABLE CONRAD LILLEY, PRESIDING JUDGE AND TO THE HONORABLE ASSOCIATE JUDGES OF THE LOS ANGELES COUNTY SUPERIOR COURT

Petitioner, ROGER JASON LEE by and through his attorney, JAMES SWANK, petitions for a writ of habeas corpus and by this verified petition states as follows

I.

Roger Jason Lee is the person on whose behalf the writ is sought, and he is presently confined and restrained of his liberty by the Department of Corrections at Chino, California.

II.

On March 15, 1981, the judgment of conviction which petitioner now challenges was entered in Los Angeles County Superior Court Number 4250005-Z.

III.

On November 16, 1980, a three-count information numbered 4250005-Z was filed in Los Angeles County Superior Court accusing defendant and petitioner Roger Jason Lee in Count One of attempting to murder Rita Daniels on September 25, 1980, in violation of Penal Code', sections 187 and 664, willfully, deliberately and with premeditation. Deadly weapon use (a knife) under section 12022, subdivision (b) and infliction of great bodily injury (GBI) under section

12022.7 were also alleged. Counts Two and Three accused petitioner with assault with a deadly weapon (section 245, subdivision (a)(1)) and robbery (section 211/212.5, subdivision (b)) with respect to the same transaction. A serious felony prior conviction (prior) was also pled. (CT 88-91.)

Petitioner was arraigned and entered pleas of not guilty to all counts on November 27, 1980, denying all enhancement allegations and the prior. (CT 91.) Jury trial

'Hereafter, unless otherwise specified, all sectional references are to the Penal Code.

[2] "CT" is petitioner's designation for Clerk's Transcript on this Petition. Petitioner hereby requests the Court to take Judicial Notice of the Clerk's Transcripts on file with this Court commenced March 11, 1981. (CT 96.) A motion to bifurcate trial on the prior conviction was granted. (CT 97) The matter was submitted to the jury on the fifth day of trial. (CT 106.) The jury returned

verdicts of guilty as to all counts and found all allegations true, specially finding that the attempted murder was committed deliberately, willfully, and with premeditation. (CT 107-108.) A court trial was then had on the prior conviction, and the court found it to be true. (CT 109.)

On April 12, 1981, petitioner was sentenced to state prison for the term prescribed by law (life with the possibility of parole) on Count One. He was further sentenced to additional terms of one and three years for the weapon and GBI enhancements, to run consecutive to the indeterminate sentence. On Count Three, the court imposed the upper term of five years, to run consecutively to the indeterminate sentence. The court imposed the upper term for Count Two, and ordered it stayed pursuant to section 654, along with the GBI and weapons enhancements charged in Count Two and Three. The court also imposed a five year term for the prior conviction. Petitioner's total unstayed prison sentence thus is fourteen years to life, with the fourteen years to be served first pursuant to section 669. (CT 198-203; RT 4/12/91, pp. 24-27.)

Notice of appeal was filed the date of sentencing. (CT 204.)[3]

3 Section III was taken from the Statement of the Case found in petitioner's opening brief on appeal, copies of which were served on the Los Angeles County Superior Court and the Los Angeles County District Attorney.

IV.

Petitioner was denied the right to effective assistance of counsel at trial guaranteed by the Sixth Amendment to the United States Constitution and by Article 1, section 15, of the California State Constitution. Petitioner's custody is illegal because petitioner's trial counsel rendered ineffective assistance of counsel in that (1) trial counsel failed to adequately investigate and prepare the case for trial; (2) trial counsel failed to properly advise petitioner of the correct maximum exposure that could result from being found guilty on all counts after a trial; (3) trial counsel failed to object to the evidence of the blood sample on the petitioner's shoe being held by the police of which the record shows had been unaccounted for during some time before the trial began; (4) trial counsel failed to attack pre-trial with either a lineup or subsequently at trial with an expert reliability of the only prosecution eyewitness/victim; and (5) said failures constituted ineffective assistance of trial counsel, thereby prejudicing petitioner.

V.

Petitioner was denied the right to effective assistance of counsel on appeal guaranteed by the Sixth Amendment to the United States Constitution and by Article 1, section 15, of the California Constitution. Petitioner's custody is illegal because petitioner's appellate counsel rendered ineffective assistance of counsel in that appellate counsel failed to raise critical and viable issues on appeal, including: (1) appellate counsel failed to argue that the evidence presented at trial was insufficient to prove a formation of a substantial basis for inference on a specific intent to kill; (2) appellate counsel failed to argue that the evidence presented at trial was insufficient to prove a reasonable finding of premeditation and deliberation; (3) appellate counsel failed to address the issues of : a) trial counsel's failure to properly investigate and prepare the case for trial, b) trial counsel's failure to properly advise petitioner of the correct maximum exposure that could result from being found guilty on all counts after trial, c) trial counsel's failure to object to the blood evidence from petitioner's shoes, and d) trial counsel's failure to properly attack the key eyewitness testimony.; and (4) said failures constituted ineffective assistance of counsel at the appellate level, thereby prejudicing petitioner.

VI.

No other applications, petitions, or motions, other than petitioner's direct appeal in F035098, have been filed in regard to petitioner's imprisonment. The particular grounds for relief alleged in this petition have not been presented in any other filed petition, application, or motion, including petitioner's direct appeal.

VII.

At trial petitioner was represented by Peter Jonas, Deputy Public Defender, 2220 Wilshire Street, Suite 300, Los Angeles, CA. 90008. On direct appeal petitioner was represented by Jay Doyle, Attorney at Law, 800 5th Street, Los Angeles, CA. 90002. This petition for writ of habeas corpus was prepared on behalf of petitioner by James Swank, Attorney At Law, 2100 Wilshire Street, Suite 505, Los Angeles, California 90008.

VIII.

This petition is addressed to the Court's original habeas corpus jurisdiction because petitioner has no other plain, speedy, or adequate remedy.

IX.

By this reference, the accompanying memorandum of points and authorities and exhibits hereto are made a part of this petition as if fully set forth herein. Petitioner's claims under this petition will be based upon the petition, the accompanying points and authorities, the exhibits attached hereto, and all records, documents and pleadings on file in *People v. Roger Jason Lee,* Los Angeles County Superior Court Case No. 425005-Z.[4]

---

[4] Petitioner asks this Court to take judicial notice of the referenced materials in its own file in Los Angeles County Superior Court Case No. 425005-Z.

WHEREFORE, petitioner respectfully requests that this Court:

1. Issue a writ of habeas corpus or an order to show cause to the Director of the Department of Corrections to inquire into the legality of petitioner's confinement;

2. If this Court concludes an evidentiary hearing is necessary in this matter, order a hearing be held before it or before a referee;

3. Issue an order vacating the judgment imposed by the Superior Court of Los Angeles County in Superior Court number 425005-Z, and further order that petitioner be returned to the trial court for further proceedings;

4. Grant petitioner such further or additional relief as may be deemed appropriate and in the interest of justice.

PETITIONER ROGER JASON LEE declares as follows:

I am the petitioner on this Petition for Writ of Habeas Corpus.

I have read the foregoing Petition for Writ of Habeas Corpus and the Memorandum of Points and Authorities in support of that Petition attached hereto, and declare that the contents of the Petition and of the Memorandum of Points and Authorities are within my knowledge, except as to those matters which are alleged therein on information and belief and as to those matters, I believe them to be true.

I certify under penalty of perjury that the foregoing is true and correct, except as to those matters alleged on information and belief and, as to those matters, I believe them to be true and correct.

Executed this 15th day of March 1992, at Chino, California.

STATEMENT OF FACTS

Rita Daniels was the night shift supervisor at the MacDonalds Restaurant at Adams and Crenshaw Streets in Los Angeles, California on September 25, 1980. She had been working there for one year and for MacDonalds Restaurants for five years. At that time, she knew petitioner as one of the employees of Ernst Steam Cleaning Company; that company cleans the vents in the broiler. Two men, one of whom would sometimes be petitioner, would come approximately once a month to do this and Ms. Daniels had seen petitioner on three to five occasions. (RT 291-293, 346-347.)[6] According to the company records, petitioner had been assigned to steam clean at that particular location on at least three occasions. (RT 400.)

Ms. Daniels was in her office doing paperwork in the early morning hours of September 25, 1980. There was no one else in the restaurant. Hearing a knock, Ms. Daniels went to see who was at the front door; she saw petitioner holding keys to the trap door to the roof. These keys had been missing since the last steam cleaners visit approximately a month before. (RT

293-295.)[7] Assuming that petitioner was returning the keys, Ms. Daniels opened the door. She said that Petitioner told her that he'd been fired, and Ms. Daniels told him that she would leave a note for her manager to see if they could get him rehired. At this point, petitioner "pulled a knife" and told her that he'd come to get his compensation. (RT 300-301.)

[5] *Statement of Facts are taken from Appellant's Opening Brief, contained in the Court Clerk's Record, and served on the Los Angeles County District Attorney previously.*

[6] *"RT" is petitioner's designation for Reporter's Transcripts on this Petition. Petitioner hereby requests the Court to take Judicial Notice of the Reporter's Transcripts on file with this Court.*

[7]*The owner of the steam cleaning service, Joe Ernst, was contacted by the restaurant with respect to the keys at 2:00 a.m. on September 11, 1980. They requested him to get in contact with his employees and determine whether one of them had picked up the keys inadvertently. On contacting petitioner, petitioner told*

Mr. Ernst that he did not have the keys to the restaurant. Mr. Ernst volunteered that he then spoke to petitioner about his past performance on other jobs, where petitioner had indicated that the job had been performed but actually had not. Mr. Ernst told petitioner that he could no longer have him service the MacDonalds Restaurants. (RT 400-403.)

Ms. Daniels turned and ran to her office, since the office door would have locked automatically if she could close it. However, the attacker caught up with her and she was unable to do so. He then directed Ms. Daniels to open the store safe, which she did. (RT 302-303.) Attacker picked up a white money bag sitting next to the safe and filled it with money from the safe. (RT 304.) Following this, attacker directed Ms. Daniels to crawl into the office. (RT 305.) Daniels crawled to the office, going to the back wall. (RT 306.) Attacker asked her to turn the light out, then slashed her throat and stabbed Daniels on the head, the back, and along her right side, inflicting thirty to forty wounds. (RT 307-308.) At one point, the blade came at Daniels's right eye, and she deflected it, breaking it; attacker continued to stab her with the handle of the knife. (RT 309-310.) Eventually, Daniels told attacker that she was tired of being stabbed, and that she was going to bleed to death anyway, so he should leave. (RT 310.) Attacker stood in the doorway, told her to wait thirty minutes since he would be watching, and then left. Daniels felt that she was going to die, so she wrote a note that Roggie from the steam cleaners done this to her.

The phone was torn off the wall, so she could not phone out. (RT 311312.)

Eventually, Ms. Daniels left MacDonalds and went to the all-night radio station located across the parking lot from the restaurant, where she got assistance. (RT 314-315.) She was in the hospital a week and has scars on her throat as a result of the incident. (RT 316.) While there, Ms. Daniels required a chest tube inserted in her thorax to expand a collapsed right lung and exploratory surgery to determine the extent of the wound to her neck. (RT 430-432.)

According to Ms. Daniels's supervisor, the total money taken from the restaurant was $356.00. (RT 450.)

Detective Ford of the Los Angeles Police Department arrested petitioner at the office of the steam cleaners in the late morning of September 25th, taking him to the police department, where he was interviewed and his "fanny pack" searched. A roll of currency was found in the fanny pack, along with over two hundred pennies and other loose change. (RT 578, 583.) During the course of the interview, petitioner told Ford that he had been at his apartment in Los Angeles with his wife and sister-in-law the previous evening. He watched television with them until approximately midnight, when he and his wife went to bed. Petitioner got up about 4:00 a.m., and he and his wife went to Denny's restaurant for breakfast. He was "real emphatic" concerning this, since he had ordered a fast breakfast which he did not have to pay for since it was not served within the ten minute limit. (RT 497-499.)

Petitioner's sister-in-law, Paula Jordan, was interviewed by Detective Ford in the afternoon of

September 25, 1980. At that time, she shared a two bedroom apartment in Los Angeles with petitioner and her sister, Mary. (RT 457-458.) The evening prior to this interview, Paula had picked up her sister at work, and they had gotten back to the apartment by 9:30 p.m. Petitioner was there, so the three of them sat down to watch television. Shortly before midnight, Mary and petitioner went to their bedroom. While she did not see petitioner leave for work around midnight, Paula assumed he had done so. This assumption stemmed from petitioner's discussion of this earlier in the evening and from vehicle headlights flashing into Paula's bedroom window shortly after midnight. (RT 460-464.) The next time she saw petitioner was shortly after 4:00 a.m., when he and Mary came to her bedroom asking her if she wanted to have breakfast with them. (RT465, 476.)[8]

A bloody shoe track was found at the scene of the assault by identification technicians processing the scene shortly afterwards. (RT 558-559.) Detective Ford obtained a search warrant for petitioner's apartment, and seized a pair of Reebok tennis

'This testimony varied from what Detective Ford testified he was told by Paula during his interview of her, which was that after petitioner and his wife went into their bedroom, Paula went into hers. After taking a shower, Paula saw petitioner in the kitchen dressed in his work clothes and shortly thereafter saw headlights illuminating her bedroom window. She looked outside and saw petitioner's truck with its lights on. Paula closed the blinds, and the lights moved away from her window and she heard the sound of a vehicle driving away. (RT 503-504.) When Ford told Paula, during the course of the interview, that petitioner had told him he had been at home all evening and asked Paula why petitioner would lie about that, Paula started to cry. (RT504-505.).'

Shoes and other items.

Comparison of the photograph of the shoe print with the shoes revealed that the measurements were the same at two points. (RT 637-638.) A small bloodstain was found on one of the shoes on a second inspection of them. (RT 639-640.)

On November 12, 1980, Detective Ford received a letter from an inmate at the Los Angeles County Jail. This letter criticized Ford for arresting the wrong person for the assault on Ms. Daniels, as someone else in the jail had done it. The person who had done it had been provided keys giving them access to the restaurant. (RT 505-508.) Ford gave the letter to identification technicians, who found what could be petitioner's right thumb print on the letter. (RT 573.) On December 10, 1980, while on the job at another location, Daniels received a letter forwarded to her from another store. (RT 332-334.) She opened it and read it. She showed the letter to her supervisors and gave it to the prosecutor's office. (RT 333-334.) This letter was from a "Roggie", who identified himself as the perpetrator. He had received the keys to MacDonalds from an accomplice who worked for "J. E.". This "Roggie" also threatened to come back and "finish ... off' Ms. Daniels if she didn't tell the police that petitioner was not the perpetrator. (RT 652-653.)

Geoff Collins, a handwriting analysis expert with the California Department of Justice, was of the opinion that the handwriting on both letters was disguised and petitioner was the probable originator of both the Ford letter and the Daniels letter. *(How could either of these letters pass review by prison mail officials? How could a threatening letter to Daniels not be caught? What were the return addresses on the letters? All letters leaving a jail or prison must have that return address.)* (RT 525, 532.)

A.

PETITIONER WAS DENIED EFFECTIVE ASSISTANCE OF COUNSEL DUE TO COUNSEL'S FAILURE TO CORRECTLY ADVISE HIM OF HIS POTENTIAL MAXIMUM EXPOSURE

In the instant case petitioner contends the failure of counsel to correctly inform and advise him of his maximum exposure under the laws to the charges he was being held to answer for constituted ineffective assistance of counsel.' As defense counsel there is clearly an obligation to correctly advise a defendant of his maximum exposure so that reasoned judgment can be exercised and together they can take the necessary steps to defend the case, and if necessary prepare for trial. Counsel's discretion in the area of trial tactics and strategy must be based upon reasonable investigation and preparation. *(Rose v. Superior Court, supra, 81* Cal. App.4th at p. 567.) There is no basis in reality that could be reasonably argued in support of this failure by counsel to even know the correct maximum exposure his client faced. Such information is fundamental to **any** criminal trial attorney's case. Petitioner did not have access to a second opinion, nor did he have access to the information or even possess the skill with which to find and correctly interpret that information. Petitioner was therefore totally reliant upon the professional ability of his appointed counsel. Since counsel was unaware of the correct exposure, he could not be expected to make any rational and informed decision on strategy and tactics founded on adequate investigation and preparation. Petitioner, however, was in no position to determine that this was, in fact, the case.

See declaration of petitioner, Exhibit A

Subsequently, through no fault of his own, neither was any decision by petitioner to proceed or not with a trial based on any possible rational and informed strategy and tactics founded on adequate investigation and preparation. In retrospect, and aside from petitioner's declaration, there is no way of knowing what decision petitioner may have made had he been properly advised of his situation. This is true not only for petitioner, but for trial counsel and the prosecution as well. This raises a reasonable probability that, but for counsel's unprofessional errors, the result of the proceeding may have been different. As such, petitioner contends that this demonstrates prejudice for which he is entitled to relief for ineffective assistance of counsel since the errors made that a reasonably competent attorney acting as a diligent and conscientious advocate would not have made sufficiently undermines confidence in the outcome.

B.

In the instant matter petitioner contends that trial counsel's failure to properly investigate and prepare the case for trial constituted ineffective assistance of counsel.

PETITIONER WAS DENIED EFFECTIVE ASSISTANCE OF COUNSEL DURING TRIAL DUE TO COUNSEL'S FAILURE TO PROPERLY INVESTIGATE AND PREPARE THE CASE FOR TRIAL

Petitioner claims he told trial counsel about stopping for gas at the time the incident took place, and provided counsel with the name and address of the gas station, along with a receipt from the gas station with the name "Harry" written on it. Along with the receipt, there is evidence that a subpoena was prepared to be delivered to "Harry"; however, it appears that the subpoena was never served, or that "Harry" was ever even contacted. (See Exhibits A, B, and C.)Trial counsel's failure to investigate a possible alibi witness had no apparent logical tactical reasoning to support it, and thus prejudiced petitioner at trial as said failure deprived petitioner of a potentially meritorious defense constituting ineffective assistance of counsel by the failure of the trial attorney to subject the case to **meaningful** adversarial testing. (See *United States v. Cronic, supra,* 466 U.S. 468 at pp. 656-657.)

In the instant case, petitioner informed his attorney that he had a possible alibi witness that 'could place him miles away from the scene of the crime at the time it took place. This is evidenced by the partially filled out subpoena. (See Exhibit C.) Yet there is no evidence that trial counsel ever attempted to locate or interview this witness. Perhaps trial counsel made a considered decision based on reasonable investigation and preparation in choosing not to attempt to locate a possible alibi witness for his client. This does not seem to be the case as we read trial counsel's own words, "We would submit that from a prosecution's standpoint, this would be considered a strong case after investigation over the last several months, the ability to present evidence to bolster my client's position has been relatively ineffectual. We would be left almost entirely without a defense were Mr. Lee to not take the stand." (RT 252.) Obviously trial counsel realized that his position was weak, and he needed all the help he could get. Additionally, as petitioner claimed he was innocent of the crime, trial counsel's stated defense position was that it was a case of **mistaken identity.** (RT 287.) To proceed to trial in such a defensive stance before completing an adequate investigation does not fall within the realm of faithful representation of the interests of a client. Trial counsel knew that even though the prosecution's case was based on only one eyewitness, there had been prior contact between the petitioner and this eyewitness; yet nothing was done to find this possible rebuttal witness for the defense of petitioner. It therefore stands to reason that trial counsel possessed no possible legitimate tactical judgment which inspired his decision to forego investigation into a possible alibi witness for his client. This relatively ineffectual ability to present evidence to bolster his client's position was due only to the fact that trial counsel failed to adequately investigate information made known to him by petitioner before the trial began.

Furthermore, petitioner raised the issue of a lack of adequate investigation before the trial proper began and was granted a Marsden Hearing. (RT 263.) The concerns of the petitioner apparently went unnoticed by trial counsel as there is no evidence that any further investigation was done. Petitioner contends this demonstrates that trial counsel was not acting as a diligent and conscientious advocate making informed choices amongst tactical alternatives such that a reasonably competent attorney would have made. Without interviewing the witness, trial counsel had no clue as to what he may or may not have said in regards to his client's whereabouts during the time in question. There is a possibility that the witness may have remembered petitioner very clearly, and that his testimony would have been convincing enough to overcome the identification of petitioner by the victim. Petitioner believes that there were enough inconsistencies in the testimony of the eyewitness as compared with her statements to police officers soon after the attack which, when coupled with the alibi witness testimony and suppression of certain evidence, would have made that possibility a reasonable one.

Because the prosecution likewise had no idea what the witness may have disclosed, they are not in any position to presume to know that but for trial counsel's unprofessional error, the result of the proceeding would not have been different.

The burden of proving guilt was on the prosecution during the trial, and their whole case rested on the eyewitness account of one person. That was when the defense should have done their investigation of this possible alibi witness, because now the burden has shifted, and it is too late for the defense to help the petitioner prove his claim of innocence. It has been twelve years since the case went to trial, and even if the alibi witness could be located now, it is unreasonable that he could remember a stranger having bought some gasoline at his place of employment that night." Even if the witness did claim to remember, it would be inconceivable that anyone would really believe him anyway. The failure of trial counsel to pursue this issue effectively waived it, leaving the petitioner without a **potentially meritorious defense** through no fault of his own. The pragmatic conclusion is that when trial counsel fails to even attempt to locate a potential alibi witness under such circumstances, the resulting prejudice should be presumed. *(Strickland v. Washington, supra,* 466 U.S. 668 at p. 690 ["Strategic choices made after less than complete investigation are unreasonable precisely to the extent that reasonable professional judgments do not support the limitations on investigations."]; *People v. Ledesma, supra,* 43 Cal.3d 171, 216; see also *In re Hall, supra,* 30 Cal.3d 408 at p. 426 [emphasizing that the exercise of counsel's professional discretion must be reasonable, informed, and founded on reasonable investigation and preparation]; *People v. Frieson, supra,* 25 Cal.3d 142 at p. 166; and *United States v. Cronic, supra,* 466 U.S. 648 at p. 659 ["...<u>if counsel entirely fails to subject the prosecution's case to meaningful adversarial testing, then there has been a denial of Sixth Amendment rights </u>that makes the adversary process itself presumptively unreliable and ... [n]o specific showing of prejudice is required..."].)

PETITIONER WAS DENIED EFFECTIVE ASSISTANCE OF COUNSE AT TRIAL BY

FAILURE OF COUNSEL TO ATTEMPT TO SUPPRESS THE EVIDENCE OF THE SHOES, WHICH THE RECORD SHOWS WERE UNACCOUNTED FOR DURING CRITICAL TIMES OF THE PROCESS OF POLICE INVESTIGATION

Petitioner contends that information showing a discrepancy in the chain of custody of the tennis shoes was available to his trial counsel, which trial counsel failed to utilize in order to attempt to have the evidence suppressed.

A pair of tennis shoes was seized from the suspect's residence approximately 10:30 a.m. September 26, 1980 by Detective Ford. (RT 592-593.) These shoes were taken by Detective Ford to police headquarters and placed on a drying rack. (RT 593.) Detective Ford made out a request that the shoes be sent to the Department of Justice and left the shoes in the custody of the Identification Bureau. (RT 593-594.) These shoes were marked as People's exhibit 53. (RT 593.)

Officer George took the shoes from the police property room to the Department of Justice lab in Los Angeles on October 3, 1980. (RT 614-615.) Officer George picked the shoes up from the Department of Justice lab and took them back to the property room on November 7, 1980. (RT 615.) Officer George again took the shoes from the property room and delivered them to the Department of Justice lab on December 13, 1980. (RT 616.) Officer George finally took the shoes back to the property room on January 8, 1981. (RT 616.) Officer George kept a record of these transport times. (RT 617.) The only time Officer George was certain the box containing the shoes was sealed was the first time he transported them. (RT 618.)

Department of Justice laboratory criminalist Bush first had contact with the shoes on October 23, 1980, according to her notes. (RT 622.) She had been asked to examine the shoes for the presence of blood. (RT 623.) She found no blood during her first examination of the shoes. (RT 625.) There were fairly large amounts of grease staining all over the shoes, the bottom, and everywhere. (RT 625.) She re-examined the shoes on

November 5th 1980. (RT 625.) Her purpose in re-examining the shoes was that it was called to her attention (by the DA after they had been in his possession) that there was a very small blood stain on the sole of the shoe. (RT 625.) She performed a species test to determine if it was actually human blood, which came out positive. (RT 626-627.) The blood appeared as a light smear on the shoe. (RT 629.) She may have missed the stain during the first examination because there was a lot of grease staining on the sole part and the stain was actually very, very small. (RT 630.) An attempt to perform an enzyme-typing test on this blood in order to determine whether this blood had come from either the suspect or the victim was unsuccessful due to the very small amount of stain. (RT 630-631.) She had been working for the Department of Justice in serology for about four and a half to five years and had qualified to testify as an expert in court probably at least a hundred times before. (RT 638.) The shoes did not appear to have been washed in any way; they were in fact very, very greasy. (RT 639.) She had conducted a very thorough test on the shoes the first time, but it may have been hard to see some areas because of the amount of grease. (RT

639.) She admitted she could have missed the stain the first time, and that it was extremely small, bordering on a trace. (RT 639.) **It is possible that the stain was not there the first time she examined them.** (Shoes were not cleaned, were covered with grease stains, could not match prints taken of tennis shoes that walked onto blood from the victim, and blood stain could not have been under grease stains during first exam.) (RT 640.)

The Physical Evidence Examination Report dated October 3, 1980, (the date that Officer George delivered the evidence). SUMMARY: "Blood was not found on the submitted pants and shoes." This report was dated at the bottom October 25, 1980, and signed by Janet Bush. (Exhibit E.) The Physical Evidence Examination Report dated December 19, 1980, (the date that Officer George delivered the evidence). SUMMARY: "As per request from Los Angeles County Deputy (sic) District Attorney, Roland LeBlanc, a stain was examined on the submitted suspect shoes. This small stain was determined to be human blood. Attempts to type this stain were unsuccessful due to an insufficient amount of sample." On page two of this report, there were two more dates;

December 28, 1980, and December 31, 1980, and the report is signed by Janet Bush. (Exhibit F.)

Relying on the above information, petitioner contends that trial counsel failed to act as a reasonably diligent advocate and without any apparent tactical reason failed to challenge the chain of custody of this critical blood evidence. Physical objects that are part of the transaction or that assist in explaining it may be introduced as evidence in the case if properly identified. *(People v. Trujillo* (1948) 32 Cal.2d 105, 115.) Before admitting any piece of physical evidence, the proponent must establish a proper chain of possession. In *People v. Lucas,* the court restated the following rules for establishing chain of custody:

The burden on the party offering the evidence is to show to the satisfaction of the trial court that, taking all the circumstances into account including the ease or difficulty with which the particular evidence could have altered, it is reasonably certain that there was no alteration. The requirement of reasonable certainty is not met when some vital link in the chain of possession is not accounted for, because then it is as likely as not that the evidence analyzed was not the evidence originally received. Left to such speculation, the court must exclude the evidence. *(People v. Lucas* (1994) 12 Cal.4th 415, 444; see also *People v. Diaz* (1982) 3 Cal.4th 495,559.)

Since Officer George testified that he had delivered the evidence (People's 53, shoes) to the lab on December 13, 1980, and the date on the report shows that they were delivered to the lab on December 19, 1980, there were approximately five or six days that the whereabouts of the shoes was unknown. Ms. Bush testified that a person had pointed out what appeared to be a very, very small bloodstain on the sole of one of the shoes, but there was no testimony indicating who that person might have been. Examining the report of December 19, 1980, we see that the prosecuting attorney, Roland LeBlanc, had requested that a small stain on one of the shoes be examined, which it was, and the stain was determined to be human blood. However, Ms. Bush had testified that the stain had been pointed out to her previous to the month of December, and that she had subsequently done a second examination of the shoe regarding this very small stain on November 5th, 1980. (RT 625.) This date seems to be confirmed in her later testimony that on November 5th, 1980, she had performed some other tests on blood from the knife found at the crime scene; in particular, she testified that "I then ran the enzyme typing that I attempted to do on the shoes." (RT 631-632.) However, the report dated October 3, 1980, shows that the knife was not delivered to the lab on that date. (Exhibit E.) In fact, the report dated December 19, 1980, shows that the knife was delivered to the lab on that date, and that the tests on the knife performed by Ms. Bush were done between December 19, 1980, and December 28, 1980. (Exhibit F.)

The contradictory nature of the testimony and the reports were confusing enough that trial counsel, had he been reviewing and organizing the information he had access to, would have been alerted to the fact that there was clearly a lapse in the continuity of the chain of possession of the tennis shoes being held by the police as evidence. Had trial counsel been alert to the record of the chain of custody and the testimony given by those involved, presumably he would have contested the introduction of the evidence. Although the record contains some evidence of the possibility that the reason trial counsel did not contest this issue on a tactical basis, (RT 695, defendant's closing argument, where trial counsel says "Well, I don't know maybe I was born yesterday, but I thought that evidence actually pointed more towards innocence.") it also contains evidence that trial counsel was aware of potential grounds for making a motion to have the evidence of the blood stain excluded. (RT 695, "You have the shoes. And I do not know if there was a blood stain on that or not. And that shows you that's --- I think that's pretty sloppy. I mean these boxes have been sitting here open all through the trial and I do not know how they keep these things.") In addition, trial counsel recognized how unusual it was that the shoes had been examined by an experienced expert who failed to find any trace of blood on the shoes until some unknown person spotted what looked to them like a trace amount of blood and the shoes were re examined. (RT 695-696.) Giving mere lip service to such an unusual occurrence during his closing did not suffice to fulfill the requirement that counsel act as a diligent advocate for his client. Considering the importance of this evidence to the prosecution's case, trial counsel should have been more diligent in challenging this critical piece of evidence. Because the record shows that the evidence was unaccounted for at critical times during the investigation process, this evidence should not have been admitted at trial. There was no way to tell from either the testimony or the records where the evidence had been or who may have had access to it during the times for which it was unaccounted for. The proper time to have addressed this issue was during the trial, when the issue of guilt or innocence was still undecided, and the burden of proving the evidence was kept securely in the hands of the correct agencies fell on the prosecution. Failure of trial counsel to address this critical issue during the trial resulted in prejudice to petitioner which constituted ineffective assistance of counsel.

STANDARD FOR REVIEWING SUFFICIENCY OF THE EVIDENCE

Petitioner acknowledges that by not raising the issue of sufficiency of the evidence on appeal, appellate counsel waived the issue for direct review and thereby prejudiced the petitioner. Therefore petitioner further argues that this is a basis for ineffective assistance of appellate counsel.

Petitioner acknowledges that the standard for review for a challenge of the sufficiency of the evidence supporting the judgment is as follows:

> "When the sufficiency of the evidence is challenged on appeal, the court must review the whole record in the light most favorable to the judgment to determine whether it contains substantial evidence, i.e. evidence that is credible and of solid value-from which a rational trier of fact could have found the defendant guilty

beyond a reasonable doubt." (*People v. Green* (1980) 27 Cal.3d 1, 55.)

"It is not [the appellate court's] function to reweigh the evidence, reappraise the credibility of the witnesses, or redetermine factual conflicts, those functions being within the province of the trier of fact." *(In re FredRogerk G.* (1979) 96 Cal. App.3d 353, 367.)

The court in *People v. Bento* (1988) 65 Cal. App.4th 179 concluded that

"The proper test for determining a claim of insufficiency of evidence in a criminal case is whether, on the entire record, a rational trier of fact could find the defendant guilty beyond a reasonable doubt." *(People v. Bento, supra,* 65 Cal. App.4th at p. 193.)On review, the court can only give credit to *"substantial"* evidence i.e., evidence that reasonably inspires confidence and is of "solid value". *(People v. Bassett* (1968) 69 Cal.2d 122, 139.; *People v. Guardado* (1994) 40 Cal. App.4th 757, 761.) The test "is equally applicable to all elements of the prosecution's *case." (Bassett, supra,* 69 Cal.2d 122 at p. 139.)

> "The critical word in the definition is `substantial'.
>
> It is a door which can lead as readily to abuse as to practical or enlightened justice. Seeking to determine the meaning of `substantial' in this connection, the court in *Estate of Teed* (1952) 112 Cal. App.2d 638, 644, canvassed dictionary and judicial definitions and concluded that the term clearly implies that such evidence must be of ponderable legal significance.
>
> Obviously the word cannot be deemed synonymous with `any' evidence. It must be reasonable in nature, credible, and of solid value; it must actually be `substantial' proof of the essentials which the law requires in a particular *case." (Bassett, Id.,* at pp. 138-139.)

The test from *Bassett* has been restated innumerable times, including in *People v. Ochoa* (1983) 6 Cal.4[h] 1199, 1206. As restated in *Ochoa,* review is to insure that the evidence reasonably inspires confidence in the judgment. *(People v. Green, supra,* 27 Cal. 3d lat p. 55.) It does not require determination of whether the evidence proves the existence of every element beyond a reasonable *doubt. (People v. Gallardo* (1984) 22 Cal. App.4`h 489, 492.) The California Supreme Court in *People v. Staten* (1980) 24 Cal.4" 343,460, reiterated the standard of review for sufficiency of evidence. The Federal Constitutional standard is the same. In *Jackson v. Virginia* (1979) 443 U.S. 307, 318-319 the United States Supreme Court held, with regard to the standard on review of the sufficiency of evidence supporting a criminal conviction, that:" [t]he critical inquiry ... [is]... whether the record evidence could reasonably support a finding of guilt beyond a reasonable doubt ... [T]his inquiry does not require a court to ask itself whether it believes that the evidence at trial established guilt beyond a reasonable doubt. Instead, the relevant question is whether, after viewing the evidence in the light most favorable to the prosecution, any rational trier of fact could have found the essential elements of the crime beyond a reasonable doubt."

An identical standard applies under the California Constitution. *(People v. Johnson* (1980) 26 Cal.3d 557, 576 .)

Despite these generalizations, several California decisions reviewing first degree murder verdicts demonstrate a tendency toward close appellate scrutiny of conflicting evidence of mental capacity, particularly where a jury's finding of capacity for premeditated murder has been made in the face of evidence in precarious balance. (See *People v. Nicolaus* (1967) 65 Cal.2d 866, 876-878; *People v. Goedecke* (1967) 65 Cal.2d 850, 857.)

In the present case, as more fully set forth below in arguments B and C, there is no credible, solid value evidence of petitioner's guilt of violation of Penal Code, section 664/187(a) (Attempted willful, deliberate, premeditated killing with malice aforethought). The failure of both trial and appellate counsel was ineffective assistance of counsel from which there is presumed prejudice. (See *In re Visciotti, supra,* 14 Cal.4th 325 at pp. 351352.)

B.

PETITIONER WAS DENIED EFFECTIVE ASSISTANCE OF COUNSEL ON APPEAL DUE TO APPELLATE COUNSEL'S FAILURE TO ARGUE THAT PETITIONER DID NOT FORM THE REQUIRED SPECIFIC INTENT TO KILL THEREBY WAIVING THE ISSUE AND PREJUDICING PETITIONER

The Court in *People v. Womack* (1994) 40 Cal. App.4th 926 concluded that "Attempted murder requires a specific intent to kill." (People *v. Womack, supra,* 40 Cal.App.4th 926 at p. 929.) In the instant case specific intent is an element of the crime of attempted murder. (See *People v. Lee* (1987) 43 Cal.3d 666, 670.)

In the instant case, there is no direct evidence that attacker had formed any specific intent beyond "compensation". (RT 301.) Nor is there any evidence

103

that this "compensation" comprised a specific intent by attacker to kill the victim. Attacker never told the victim he was going to kill her. As set forth in *People v. Falck* (1997) 52 Cal. App.4th 287 "The element of intent is rarely susceptible of direct proof and must usually be inferred from all facts and circumstances disclosed by evidence." *(People v. Falck, supra,* 52 Cal. App.4th 287 at p. 299.)

The court in *People v. Keister* (1986) 46 Cal. App.4th 1318 concluded that:

> "(a)cts will be sufficient to constitute attempt to commit crime when they clearly indicate certain, unambiguous intent to that specific crime, and in themselves, are an immediate step in present execution of criminal *design".(People v. Keister, supra,* 46 Cal. App.4th 1318 at p. 1323.)

In the instant case the record indicated that there was nothing to stop the attacker from attempting further injury or death. Here the attacker abandoned the criminal act instead of consummating the act of murder. In determinating petitioner's intent regard should be given to what occurred at the time of the attempted killing, as well as to what was done before and after that time. (See *People v. Eggers* (1947) 30 Cal.2d 676, 686.) In fact, the record shows that the attacker told the victim to wait thirty minutes because he would be watching. (CT 28; RT 311.) If the attacker had formed the specific intent to kill the victim, there was nothing preventing him from doing so. The victim testified that there were other knives in the restaurant. (RT 372.) Obviously the attacker did not believe that the victim was going to bleed to death, or else there would have been no reason to tell her to wait 30 minutes. The evidence does not exist that the attacker had the requisite degree of knowledge to determine that the victim would die of blood loss in a short amount of time. If the attacker had thought the victim was going to live and be able to identify him, there was no reason not to go ahead and kill her if he had already formed the specific intent to do so.

It is well established that criminal intent can rarely, if ever, be shown by statements or testimony of the petitioner, but may be manifested by the circumstances connected with the offense. (See *People v. Murphy* (1943) 60 Cal. App.2d 762, 770.)

The applicable test from a conviction of the crime of attempt is whether there is substantial evidence to support the finding that petitioner committed some act which unequivocally manifested an existing intention to go forward to completion of the crime thus intended. (See *People v. Lyles* (1957) 156 Cal. App.2d 482, 486.) In the instant case, the evidence was insufficient on this issue. The failure of appellate counsel to raise this issue was constitutionally deficient.

C.

PETITIONER WAS DENIED EFFECTIVE ASSISTANCE OF COUNSEL ON APPEAL DUE TO FAILURE OF APPELLATE COUNSEL TO ARGUE THAT THE RECORD LACKS SUFFICIENT EVIDENCE TO ESTABLISH EXPRESS MALICE BEYOND A REASONABLE DOUBT

Penal Code, section 188 defines malice as: "... express or implied. It is express when there is manifested a deliberate intention unlawfully to take away the life of a fellow creature. It is implied when no considerable provocation appears, or when the circumstances attending the killing show an abandoned and malignant heart." In order to refine and clarify this definition, one Court has said that: "Express malice consists of specific intent to kill, i.e., manifestation of deliberate intention unlawfully to take away the life of a fellow creature." *(In re Sergio R.* (1981) 228 Cal. App.3d 588, 595.)

In the instant case petitioner was convicted of the crime of attempted first degree murder. Attempted murder requires **express malice, i.e. specific intent to**

kill, which is a requisite element of the crime, and mere implied malice is an insufficient basis on which to sustain such a charge. (See *People v. Lee, supra,* 43 Cal.3d 666 at p. 670; *People v. Carpenter* (1987) 15 Cal.4`ⁿ 312, 391.)

The court in *People v. Knapp* (1886) 71 Cal. 1 concluded that "When no provocation appears from the evidence given by the prosecution, malice is implied, and the killing with malice is unlawful".(People v. *Knapp, supra,* 71 Cal. 1 at p.11.)In the present case the record lacks any evidence of "considerable provocation" as stated in Penal Code, section 188, by the victim directed at the petitioner. Of course, malice **may** be implied from felonious assault without justification or mitigating circumstances. (See *People v. Roberts* (1975) 51 Cal. App.3d 125.) However, since no showing of considerable provocation exists in the record, the only reasonable conclusion which can be drawn is that where there is nothing to show provocation or justification for homicide, the malice **must** be implied. (See *People v. Cole* (1956) 47 Cal.2d 99, 106; *People v. Alvarado* (1981) 232 Cal. App.3d 501, 504-505.) That is the case here. The only possible malice that may have existed was implied malice. However, **attempted murder requires express malice; it requires a specific intent to kill,** which was not present in the instant *case. (See People v. Carpenter, supra,* 15 Cal.4th 312; see also argument B, infra.)

The prosecution made their case based on the facts that petitioner had worked at the restaurant previously, and because of his being prohibited from servicing that particular restaurant, for which he blamed the victim, he attempted to kill her as part of his plan of revenge. (RT 661-662.) There was no evidence presented that the petitioner (or attacker) had formed any express malice prior to going to the restaurant and robbing the money from the safe. The victim was not physically harmed during the robbery. It was only after the victim was unable to comply with the demand to open the other safe that any attack took place. (CT 18-22.) This inability to comply did not indicate the presence of considerable provocation by the victim, nor any justification for the attack. Therefore, the evidence of express malice could only have come from the act of the attempted murder itself. There was no evidence presented that the attacker told the victim at any time during the attack that he was going to kill her. And that act in itself was insufficient to establish the requisite element of express malice, as there was no manifestation during that act of a deliberate and specific intention to kill. The attacker terminated the attack in progress and left the victim alive and with instructions to not call the police for at least thirty minutes. He had every opportunity to inflict the final "coup de gras" but deliberately left his victim alive and with every expectation that she would live. This act did not imply malice. *(People v. Knapp, supra, 71* Cal. I at *p. 7.)*

In conclusion, the record contains absolutely no significant evidence of the **express malice** with which petitioner (or attacker) must have acted in order for a conviction of attempted first degree murder to be justified and proved beyond a reasonable doubt. Because appellate counsel failed to meet the obligation to "raise crucial assignments of error that arguably could have resulted in reversal" on appeal, petitioner was denied effective assistance of counsel on appeal. *(People v.*

Lang, supra, 11 Cal. 3d at p.142; see also *In re Harris, supra, 5* Cal.4th at pp.832-834.) Said failure resulted in prejudice to petitioner, as the total lack of any argument did not subject the case to any meaningful adversarial process.

PETITIONER WAS DENIED EFFECTIVE ASSISTANCE OF COUNSEL ON APPEAL DUE TO APPELLATE COUNSEL'S FAILURE TO ARGUE THAT THE EVIDENCE WAS INSUFFICIENT TO FORM A REASONABLE FINDING OF PREMEDITATION AND DELIBERATION

Petitioner acknowledges that appellate counsel failed to raise the issue of whether the evidence was insufficient to form a reasonable finding of premeditation and deliberation on appeal. While this issue may be directly waived by appellate counsel's defect, the failure itself raises the further issue of ineffective assistance of counsel on appeal. The court in *People v. Anderson* (1968) 70 Cal.2d 15, gave us the standard for review of when premeditation and deliberation exists. The court stated that:

"The type of evidence which this court has found sufficient to sustain a finding of premeditation and deliberation falls into three basic categories:(1) facts about how and what defendant did *prior to* the actual killing which show that the defendant was engaged in activity directed toward, and explicable as intended to result in, the killing- what may be characterized as planning activity; (2) facts about the defendant's *prior* relationship and/or conduct with the victim, which inference of motive, together with facts of type (1) or (3), would in turn support an inference that the killing was the result of a pre-existing reflection" and "careful thought and weighing of considerations" rather than "mere unconsidered or rash impulse hastily executed"...; (3) "facts about the nature of the killing from which the jury could infer that the manner of killing was so particular and exacting that the defendant must have intentionally killed according to a `preconceived design' to take his victim's life in a particular way for a reason which the jury can reasonably infer from facts of type (1) or (2)."(People *v. Anderson, supra,70* Cal.2d 15 at pp. 26-27.)

Moreover, the court in *People v. Lucero* (1988) 44 Cal.3d 1006, 1018 citing *People v. Alcala* (1984) 36 Cal.3d 604, 627 concluded that the planning is "the most important prong" and more recently it has been held that the pertinent categories of evidence bearing on premeditation and deliberation are: 1) planning activity; 2) motive; and 3) manner of killing. (See *People v. Garcia* (1980) 78 Cal. App.4th 1422, 1427.)

In the present case there is no evidence to show that petitioner planned to kill the victim. He was known by the victim from previous encounters with her at the restaurant while he was there to clean the vents. The victim recognized him, and would be able to easily identify him to the police. Yet, attacker wore no disguise in order to mask his appearance from the victim. This is certainly not evidence that anything was planned, but rather that petitioner, **if it was him**, was acting on a rash impulse basis when he attacked the victim. If in fact the plan was to kill the victim, it would

113

be unreasonable under the circumstances to assume that the victim would have been left alive.

In addition to the above, trial counsel had further evidence at his disposal that would have bolstered his argument that petitioner never neither premeditated nor deliberated. Vincent Mouton, the late night disc jockey from the radio station located to the north of the restaurant told Officer Frausto that it was unusual for Ms. Daniels to be at the restaurant so late, and that she usually leaves about 1:00 a.m. (See Exhibit H.) Supporting this statement further was the statement of the store manager, Malik Barak, made to Officer Metoyer that Ms. Daniels was supposed to have left the store with the rest of the night shift crew. (See Exhibit I.) Obviously the petitioner, who had worked on a regular basis at the restaurant knew that Ms. Daniels usually left about 1:00 a.m. then it would be logical to presume (and therefore examine on this point) that petitioner did not enter the premises with the intention of finding Ms. Daniels there and killing her.' [1]

The second requirement per *Anderson* in order for the existence of premeditation and deliberation is the

114

motive. It is well established that the absence of motive tends to support the presumption of innocence and it is a fact to be reckoned on the side of innocence. (See *People v. Albertson,* (1944) 23 Cal.2d 550, *567; People v. Weatherford* (1945) 27 Cal.2d 401, 423; and *People v. Planagan* (1944) 65 Cal. App.2d 371, 403.) While there is a motive in the instant case, the only motive shown by the evidence for the attack was to gain compensation, or revenge, for being fired caused by previous actions of the victim. This motive lacks sufficient strength to establish the presence of premeditation or deliberation of an attempted murder, as the evidence shows that petitioner **was still working**, and had only been taken off the work from that particular restaurant, not all of them. (RT 392-393.) The loss of a single job out of many is insufficient evidence to support a reasonable finding of attempted murder.

Finally the last requirement per *Anderson* is the manner of killing. In the instant case a small knife was used to attack the victim. While said knife could certainly have caused the death of the victim, petitioner argues that had the intent to kill been present, along with premeditation, a larger and stronger knife would have made more sense. The knife used broke during the attack, thus rendering it useless for killing. This supports a finding that attacker did not premeditate and deliberate any attempt to kill, only to threaten the victim with assault in order to gain her cooperation in opening the safes. The failure of both trial and appellate counsel to even attempt to raise this issue under the circumstances constituted ineffective assistance of counsel.

"These matters were never brought out at trial by counsel. Hence it would not have appeared "on the record" and appellate counsel would not have known to raise these points on appeal. It is again for this reason that a Habeas Petition is more suited to raising such an ineffective assistance of counsel matter. *(People v. Pope, supra,* 23 Cal.3d 412 at p. 426; *People v. Torres* (1979) 96 Cal. App.3d 14.)

PETITIONER WAS DENIED EFFECTIVE ASSISTANCE OF COUNSEL ON APPEAL DUE TO APPELLATE COUNSEL'S FAILURE TO ARGUE THE ISSUE OF THE IMPROPER IDENTIFICATION PROCEDURE EMPLOYED BY POLICE

Petitioner contends that the procedure used for the initial identification of the suspect in the instant case was improper and the issue should have been raised on appeal. The record reflects that on Sept. 25, 1980, two Polaroid photographs were taken of petitioner by an I. Bureau Technician. (RT 586.) These two photos were then taken to the hospital by Detective Ford and shown to the victim, who at the time was in the intensive care unit. (RT 586-587.) At the time, Detective Ford believed the victim was going to survive the assault. (Exhibit G, p. 7 of 13.) According to the physician on duty in the emergency room, the victim was in stable condition when she arrived at the hospital. (RT 430.) According to the discharging physician, the victim would have been able to return to work after a couple of weeks. (RT 439.) The victim had just gotten out of surgery when Detective Ford showed her the photos. (RT 365.) There were no other photos taken or shown to the victim by Detective Ford. (RT 366, 598.) Detective Ford was familiar with the term "photographic lineup". (RT 598.) Detective Ford admitted to not having used the procedure of showing six photos to the victim. (RT 599.) Detective Ford testified that the victim did not have her eyeglasses on at any time during this identification process, and that she had asked her daughter to obtain the eyeglasses and bring her a pair. (RT 599.) The victim testified that she needed to wear her eyeglasses in order to see to write. (RT 364.) The victim testified that without her glasses she would have difficulty identifying the suspect. (RT 367.) The victim testified that when she was talking to Police Officers at the hospital, she was wearing an oxygen mask. (RT 358.) Detective Ford testified that the victim appeared to be in a lot of pain. (RT 599.) Detective Ford testified that the victim was breathing very heavily, that she was hooked up to a chest tube, her neck was in a brace, and her hands were shaking. (RT 603.) Detective Ford testified that her hands were

118

shaking so much; he had to hold the photographs in order for her to be able to see them. (RT 604.)

There is obviously no reason to doubt that the victim was convinced that she knew who had attacked her. This does not necessarily mean that she was correct. It was around 3:00 a.m., she was alone, and working later than usual, so she was probably tired. (RT 294; Exhibit I.) She was working in the office doing paperwork when she heard a knock on the door. (RT 293-294.) She required eyeglasses in order to do the paperwork she was involved with. (RT 322.) It was dark outside except for the lights in the parking lot. (RT 298, 299.) The lights inside had been dimmed considerably. (RT 349.) The people who do the cleaning show up during these hours. (RT 347.) They were due to come back any day. (RT 350.) She went to see who was at the door, and saw someone standing there holding up a set of keys which looked to be the ones that had turned up missing about a month earlier. (RT 294.) She assumed the person was there to return the keys. (RT 299.) She assumed the person was there to clean the floors. (Exhibit G, p. 8 of 13.) She opened the door and the person with the keys told her he had been fired. (RT 300.) She asked him what his first name was, to which he replied "Roggie." (RT 300.) Now, at that point, she had no reason not to believe what she had been told by the person. After all, she had seen Roger around the restaurant before, and knew he was a young black man. She had talked to Roger's employer about the missing keys, and she and the employer had come to the conclusion that Roger had, in fact, been the one who had taken them even though there was no evidence to support that conclusion. She knew his first name. She was worried about what Roger might do if he found out that she was mainly responsible for getting him fired. However, had he been fired? He was arrested at the workplace. She had no reason to expect Roger to show up except to do some wrong. (Exhibit H, p. 4 of 7.) In light of all this, some substantial questions come to mind. Why did she open the door for someone she believed she had reason to fear? Why did she ask his name if she knew him and recognized him? Was she wearing her glasses at the time? Why did she think he was there to clean the place since she believed she was responsible for getting him fired from working at that restaurant? The most reasonable conclusion is that she did not recognize the person as Roger; in fact, she thought it was someone else at first; someone from the cleaning company who was there to work, and had brought back the missing keys. It was only after hearing this person say he had been fired, and his name was Roggie, that she reached the conclusion that this was the man whom she feared would do her harm if he found out she had been responsible for getting him fired. This assumption was further supported by him telling her that he had come for compensation and the sudden appearance of a knife in his hand. (RT 301.) In fear, she ran toward the office for protection. (RT 301.) She was followed by the man, who stopped her from gaining access to the office and closing the door. (RT 301-302.) With the knife in his hand, he told her to open the safe. (RT 302-303.) At that point, it would be reasonable to assume that she was terrified, and convinced that this was the same man who she was afraid of. Had Detective Ford provided her with more photos of different young black men, or had a proper lineup been done, it may well have turned out that she would have been unable to pick out the suspect or possibly she would have picked out someone else altogether. Cross racial identifications are always suspect, with very good reason. Petitioner contends that under the totality of these circumstances it could well have been any young black male that came near to fitting his physical size that the victim saw and was attacked by that night. **There was never any other description given by the victim other than young, black, man". (Exhibit** G at pp. 8, 9 of 13.) There was no attempt made by police to gather any further description from the victim before showing her the photos of the person she believed was responsible. Petitioner contends that these facts establish conclusively that a reasonable probability has been demonstrated that the results of a proper photographic line up could have at least provided some doubt in the victim's mind of the identification of the suspect, and/or the jury's as well. The procedure utilized by the police for purposes of pre-trial identification were unfairly suggestive and denied petitioner of his Constitutional guarantee of due process.

It is the likelihood of misidentification which violates a defendant's right to due process. We turn, then, to the central questions, whether under the "totality of circumstance" the identification was reliable even though the confrontation procedure was suggestive. *(Neil v. Biggers* (1972) 409 U.S. 188, 93 S. Ct. 375, 34 L. Ed. 2d 401.) The factors to be considered in evaluating the likelihood of misidentification include "the opportunity of the witness to view the criminal at the time of the crime, the witness' degree of attention, the accuracy of the witness' prior description of the criminal, the level of certainty demonstrated by the witness at the confrontation, and the length of time between the crime and the confrontation." *(Neil v. Biggers, supra,* 93 S. Ct. 375 at p. 382.)The witness testified that she had been wearing her eyeglasses during the attack. (RT 322.) The witness testified that she had been wearing her glasses while viewing the photographs of the suspect. (RT 367.) Detective Ford testified that she was not wearing her glasses while viewing said photographs. (RT 599; Exhibit G, page 9 of 13.) The witness' recollection and testimony may be regarded as suspect in light of such contradictory testimony. Furthermore, the witness' glasses appeared in a photograph taken of the crime scene which showed them situated in blood, lying on the desk in the office where the attack took place. (RT 321.) The witness clearly took her glasses off after writing the note and left them on her desk. Under the circumstances, this presents a strong indication that the witness had a reflective habit of taking off her glasses when leaving her desk, and raises a reasonable doubt as to whether or not she was wearing them at the time of the attack. To the extent that it is unknown whether the witness was wearing her eyeglasses at the time of the crime, it is uncertain as to what degree of opportunity she was afforded the viewing of the suspect by the witness during that time. While trial counsel failed to establish for the record the exact nature of her sight disability, she needed her glasses to do her work in the office. (RT 321-322.) Additionally, the lighting was very low in the area of the safe, which was close to the floor, making it difficult for the witness to see exactly what the suspect was doing while the suspect was squatting down taking the money from the safe. (RT 362-363.) The witness testified that she had been lying flat on the floor on her stomach during the time the suspect was taking the money from the safe. (RT 338.) There was one light on in the office, and it was not very bright. (RT 307.) During the time in the office the witness was being stabbed from behind while she was on her hands and knees, indicating that she had no real opportunity to view the suspect at that time. (RT 308.) The witness testified that she got a good look at the suspect after he stopped stabbing her, when she turned around to tell him he could stop stabbing her and go, because he was standing right in the light of the office door for thirty seconds to a minute. (RT 364-365.) This testimony was in direct contradiction to her earlier testimony that he was still stabbing her when she said that to him. (RT 310.) Although the witness testified that she could see the suspect through her glasses unimpaired in spite of the blood running down them, she found it necessary to clean and put on her glasses before writing the note after the attack. (RT 311, 364-365.)

The witness was unable to testify as to what kind of clothing was worn by the suspect, what color they were, if the suspect had been wearing gloves, or if the suspect had any facial hair. (RT 355-356.) In fact, the only thing the witness was able to say about the physical appearance of the suspect was that the suspect was "young, black, male". This does not evince facts that the witness was very observant of anything in particular about the suspect, which was most likely due to the fact that she had already made up her mind about who the suspect was. Furthermore, the witness was unable to say exactly when or how the telephone was taken from the office. (RT 312.)

The witness' prior description was limited to "**young, black, male**". This description did nothing to distinguish the suspect from millions of other individuals, and therefore supported nothing beyond that description by which a reasonable identification of the suspect may have been made.

As the witness had just come from surgery prior to viewing the photos, and because of the level of injuries sustained by the witness, it was reasonable to assume that she was under the influence of at least one powerful medication. That in itself should have been enough to cast substantial doubt on the reliability of the identification, but here we had the additional facts that she was not wearing her eyeglasses, and the cross-racial nature of the identification.

That the witness was able to identify the suspect with certainty from the profile photograph, in the condition she was in, without her glasses, should have given counsel cause for pause. (Exhibit G, p. 9 of 13.) Considering her lack of attention to the appearance of petitioner during the initial contact the night of the crime, and to her subsequent assumptions made at the time of the crime as to the identity of the suspect, a reasonable probability existed that had the victim been shown other photographs of different individuals, the outcome of her identification could have been much different.

Under the totality of circumstances, the unreliability of the pre-trial identification of the suspect would have been obvious by trial counsel's complete and thorough inquiry into all circumstances to prove invalidity. Trial counsel was in an excellent position to make a prima facie case that the procedures fell short of the required due process. Trial counsel knew of the critical nature of the identification yet he did nothing pre-trial to test its reliability. Trial counsel should have made a motion to suppress the evidence of the tainted photo identification in an attempt to force the burden of proof onto the prosecution. The prosecution would then have had to show that the in-court identification had an independent source or origin by clear and convincing evidence. Considering that the whole case of the prosecution rested on the eyewitness identification issue, there could have been no rational trial tactic for the failure of the trial attorney to put the issue to a meaningful adversarial test. There is nothing in the record indicating that any other pre-trial identification was sought. During the in-court identification, the witness identified the suspect as the man sitting next to the defense attorney. (RT 295.) The witness knew who was on trial, she knew who the defense attorney was, and where he was sitting, she knew the defendant would be the person sitting next to the defense attorney. At the time she was asked to identify the suspect in court, she had only to make an assumption, not any reliable identification. Had some other young, Black male been sitting next to the defense attorney, she would have possibly identified him as her attacker, even with her glasses on her face. Both the pretrial and in-court confrontations were so arranged as to make the resulting identifications virtually inevitable.

Accordingly, trial counsel should have made a motion to suppress the tainted pre-trial identification, as well as an objection to the subsequent in-court identification, but failed to do so. (RT 295.) Said failure to object waived the issue on appeal and forces petitioner now to raise it by way of the instant Habeas Petition.

Nowhere in the record does it indicate any reason for not following standard police procedure and utilizing a photographic lineup. Nowhere in the record is it indicated that the victim was in any danger of not surviving the attack after her initial medical treatment. Her condition was stated as "stable yet critical" by Detective Ford in his report on his interview with the victim. (Exhibit G at p. 13 of 13.) Detective Ford had told petitioner that he understood the victim was in serious condition but that she was apparently going to survive the attack. (Exhibit G at p. 7 of 13.) If the victim was is such danger of death as to allow the identification procedure utilized by Detective Ford, then there was no reason for him to wait so long after he had the suspect in custody to take the pictures and show them to the victim. And if there was no great need for speed in the identification process, then there was no need to take the photos and show them to the victim at a time when the victim was obviously in no condition to reliably identify any such photos. She had just gotten out of surgery, and was undoubtedly under the influence of some pain medications, such as morphine, or some other powerful narcotic. Her vision was blurry enough to require her to wear her eyeglasses when she wrote the note indicating who had attacked her, yet Detective Ford testified that she did not have her glasses available at the time she was asked to make the identification. She was in a great deal of pain, and had an oxygen mask partially blocking her vision. Her hands were shaking so badly she could not hold the photos still enough to look at them. Yet, here was a police officer asking her, "Is this the guy?" while showing her only two photos of the person she was already convinced was responsible. If everyone was so sure of whom the responsible party was, and that the victim would have been able to identify him, then there was no reason **not** to follow the standard police procedure utilizing a photographic lineup. Because the prosecution's case rested entirely on one eyewitness, trial counsel's failure to properly attack and rebut this

130

evidence is not within the bounds of any sound and carefully considered tactical maneuver. Appellate counsel should have raised this argument on appeal. The failure of both constitutes ineffective assistance of counsel at both trial and appellate levels.

CONCLUSION

For all of these reasons, and in the interest of justice, petitioner respectfully requests that this petition be granted.

Roger Jason Lee still is incarcerated. The Writ was completed and there were high hopes that a retrial or release would be granted. On March 27, 1992, the Superior Court Judge rendered his decision. Denial was based on potential overwhelming evidence of guilt and that the Writ was <u>not</u> submitted in a timely manner. The judge would not rule on the writ attorney's advice that the petitioner nor his parents could afford the twenty-five thousand dollars to investigate the case and the trial proceedings during a period which could be considered timely. The ruling of the judge is as follows:

Petitioner on Habeas Corpus

Having reviewed the petition for writ of habeas corpus dated March 17, 1992, and filed on March 19, 1992, the Court finds that existing evidence does not justify the requested relief at this time.

First, petitioner has not been diligent. According to underlying case No. 4250005-Z, petitioner was sentenced for attempted murder and related charges on April 12, 1981. The judgment was affirmed by the Third Appellate District in an opinion dated May 26, 1982. In 1988, petitioner unsuccessfully sought to have sentence recalled. On March 21, 1990, the Third Appellate District once again affirmed the judgment in this case. Thus, petitioner's belated assertions of ineffective assistance of counsel are of questionable merit. (See, e.g., *In re* Clark (1983)a claim bars consideration of the merits of the petition for writ of habeas corpus], Augustine v. *Superior Court* (1989) 71 Cal. App. 4th 990 [a convicted defendant is not entitled to seek relief by way of habeas corpus at defendant's leisure, but must act expeditiously or risk rejection for unexplained untimeliness], and In *re Ronald* E. (1977) 19 Cal.3d 315 [lack of diligence can result in a waiver of any constitutional defects alleged by way of petition for writ of habeas corpus]; cf. *Carey v.* Saffold (1982) 536 U.S. 214, 122 S.Ct. 2134 [federal habeas corpus petitions must be filed within one year and California petitions must be filed within a "reasonable" time].) This is especially true when the petition asserts ineffective assistance of counsel. (Cf. *Bonin v. Calderon* (9th Cir. 1986) 77

F.3d 1155 and *McCleskey v.* Zant (1981) 499 U.S. 467.)

Second, ineffective assistance of counsel requires not only deficient representation, but resulting prejudice to the petitioner. (See, e.g., *Lockhart* v. Fretwell (1983) 506 U.S. 364, 113 S.Ct. 838, *Strickland v. Washington* (1984) 466 U.S. 668, *In re* Ross (1985) 10 Cal.4th 184, and *People v. Lewis (1990)* 50 Cal-3d 262.) However, as noted in the opinions issued by the Third Appellate District in appeals F015785 and F035137 and in the record in the underlying case, there is abundant evidence of the petitioner's guilt. Furthermore, petitioner affirms his guilt in the declaration he provided in support of this petition.

(See Exh. A, ₁ 5 ["Had I known the actual potential consequence, I would not have proceeded to trial"].) By stating that he would have accepted a plea to a lower term, petitioner is effectively refuting any assertion of innocence.

(Cf. *People v. Halstead* (1985) 175 Cal. App..3d 772 [a guilty plea waives any rights to raise questions regarding the evidence, including its sufficiency or admissibility, whether or not subsequent claims of error are based on alleged constitutional violations], *People v. Bonwit* (1985) 173 Cal.App.3d 828 [a guilty plea is more than an admission of guilt, it is a waiver of affirmative defenses], and *Kercheval v. United States* (1927) 274 U.S. 220 [a guilty plea is itself a conviction and is conclusive].)

Further consideration of this matter is not warranted. The petition is denied.

DATED this 21ST day of March 1992.

Court appointed attorneys during the trial and in the Appellate Courts hearings did not have the financial resources to investigate the case and trial, as did the Writ attorney. The Writ was filed with the judge on March 19 and it took him two days to render his decision. The judge's ruling citing the Appellate Courts' findings which have none of the findings discovered by the Writ attorney prejudiced his decision against the petitioner.

Roger Jason Lee can only pray that one day he will be paroled.

THE END

B.

AFTERWORDS

By Roger Jason Lee

Following is a later Writ explaining the theory surrounding Mr. Roger Thierry and written by Roger Jason Lee and a new attorney in addition to Mr. Lee's observations and first-hand knowledge of actions taken by officials and the victim.

**PETITIONER
OBJECTION TO
"FACTUAL AND
PROCEDURAL
HISTORY"
(A. The Crimes)**

Petitioner objects to the inaccurate statement of facts and procedural history as the respondent has manipulated the record as follows:

The Police Report states the victim heard a knock at the side door, not the front door. Also, it is in error to state that the victim saw petitioner five times prior to the crime when he only serviced that place 3 times over several months (RT 398-399). Should an evidentiary hearing be held Joe Ernst. (See respondents (4) Footnote. Also, Mr. Ernst will testify that all employees were given a roof hatch key to all MacDonalds. Restaurants, so petitioner had no need to ask

138

for the keys let alone take them. Ms. Daniels assumed Roger Thierry was returning the keys as Thierry admits to in his confession. Petitioner was never fired which leaves no motive (RT 410-41 2)

Thierry admits via his confession that he was in fact fired. (Petitioner Ex. 'e')

Thierry has the same first name as petitioner and this was the reason Ms.

Daniels was confused as to who did this to her. (Petitioner Ex. 'e') Thierry states in his confession that he pulled out a screwdriver and that he never came there with a knife.

Ms. Daniels states in the police report that she knew the suspect and even states she was afraid of petitioner 2 weeks earlier when the keys in question came up missing. She states she got a phone call from a bogus alarm company, and that she believed it was petitioner checking to see if a burglary could take place and that she was afraid of petitioner ever since. But on the night in question she opens the door not to a person she is afraid of but to Thierry, and she asked for his name, which means it wasn't petitioner and she really did not know who the person was.

Respondent makes it seem as victim was humiliated by being made to crawl to the office. Well now we know that Thierry crawled behind the victim to escape detection something that we didn't know (**Petitioner**. Ex. 'C') If

Joe Ernst thought petitioner had taken the keys he would have been fired, but he was not fired. It should be noted that all the employees of Joe Steam Cleaning were asked about the keys and this will be verified by Mr. Ernst at the evidentiary hearing.

Also the victim stated suspect stabbed her first, then changed her Story, saying the knife broke and then Thierry continued to stab her. (RT

306-310). The knife was already broke at this point and the handle of the knife could not have made the small puncture wounds that were superficial. (RT428-429)

According to Thierry he used a screwdriver and did not bring it with him, the knife that is. But he found the knife on the counter (**Petitioner** Ex. 'C')

The screwdriver is consistent with the victims wounds. Note that the records shows blood was allover the office but not on petitioner. (PR pg. 1 of 5)

Thierry states he had a friend with him and that he told the victim that she would not die and he and his friend looked around for 20 minutes So the victim couldn't have waited 10 minutes as she states (RT 311-312)The victim did not have her glasses on during the assault as they were left on the desk, making it difficult for her to give an accurate report of the suspect **1.0**. (RT 311).

Thierry states he saw in the fact that he and the petitioner have the same name as a means to use petitioner as a scapegoat for his crimes. The respondent misleads this court yet again stating that the victim was stabbed by the knife handle, when the victim could not **1.0** the knife. (RT 646) The victim states "it was to dark." but at this same dark period she claims she can't describe the suspect because she was looking at the knife. She states (PR from this point on represents Police Report) to officer Stillwagon that 'it was dark.' (PR pg. 4 of 7) How then can she I.D. any suspect? "Because the restaurant itself was dark." (RT 647) Again the victim was afraid of petitioner so why open the door if she knew it was him? Because it wasn't. She stated she was informed that petitioner was fired and she was responsible. But why open the door to someone you she had fired? Because it was Thierry not petitioner, and again petitioner was never fired.

(RT 41 0-41 2). The victim says she handed money to the suspect, so he didn't take it. (RT 648)

No matching knife was ever located at petitioners house nor connected to him. (PR 12 of 13) Neither of the shoe tracks watched petitioner or victim showing Thierry did have a third party there. (RT 545, 558-559)

PETITIONER OBJECTS TO 5B "OTHER EVIDENCE Linking Petitioner To The Crime"

Petitioner was never advised of his Miranda Rights. <u>Miranda v. Arizona</u> (1966) 384 U.S. 436. It was easy for Detective Stokes to insert this advisement into the record as their were no witnesses that he ever read petitioner his rights. (RT 496)

Petitioner shoes were measured but not accurately. (RT 495-496)

It could be 10' inches for all we know, and blood was not there the first time they were tested. (RT 640)

$444.00 was taken from the crime scene and yet petitioner only had $56.05. (RT 580) The respondent misstates facts saying petitioner had "twenty $5 bills. (PR pg. 6,7 of 13; 12 of 13)None of the items found in petitioners fanny pack were even remotely related to the crime. And petitioners sister-in-law could not have stated she went to her bedroom to shower, as there was no shower in her bedroom. (RT503) Detective Ford assumed there was blood on petitioner's shoes which proved later to be negative for blood. (Petitioner Ex **'B'** pg. 7) Respondent fails to mention that initially no blood was found on the shoe. The respondent out-right lies when he says that blood was found on the shoe and was consistent with Ms. Daniels's blood type. (RT 632-633) The blood on the knife was consistent with the victim, not with petitioners shoe. (RT 631-633)

The shoe tracks were not identified as being them same. (RT 635) This is another outright lie and falsification of documents. Also Thierry was in the county jail the same time as respondent but not, in the same pod. Thierry was there under an alias 'Roggie' on an unrelated charge. When an evidentiary hearing is held Thierry will be called to testify to this. (RT 635-638)

The respondent again tried to mislead this court. The criminalist could not determine that petitioner's shoes were the same as the suspects. (RT 640-642) Detective Stokes testified that the victim was not wearing her glasses when trying to I.D. petitioner in photos, The prosecution indicates that the police reports are inaccurate because the victim was under heavy stress and pain. If this is so then it backs up what the victim said in trial about not knowing faces. (RT 431).

Dr. Harmon states the victim had small wounds, which is consistent with Thierry's use of a screwdriver, in addition she states it was upwards of 32 small puncture wounds not 30-40. (RT 436) The victims small puncture wounds were not sutured, which is consistent with Thierry's use of a screwdriver (RT 437). Victim's wounds other than her throat and chest were all superficial.

Petitioners print was on the letter from Thierry/Roggie because Detective Ford came to the county jail and handed it to the petitioner and asked him if he wrote it. That's why only one print was found. When an evidentiary hearing is held Detective Stokes will testify to this fact, and subpoenaed copies of the jail visiting logs will be on hand.

(PL stands for Preliminary Hearing)

The letter from Crazy E/Thierry is consistent with Thierry's confession that he did it for drugs and to take a trip to New Zealand. (Petitioner Ex 'C') Petitioner's blood was tested and was negative for drugs and alcohol and has never used drugs. Petitioner was also sent a letter from Crazy

E/Thierry and petitioners trial attorney failed to use it, but attorney Peter Jones will be called to testify to this at the evidentiary hearing.

Mr. Collins stated something totally different in his report. (RT 526-528) Mr. Collins states: 'He could not conclude that the same person authored both letters. Again respondent is trying to mislead this court. Geoff Collins confirms his original report saying: 'he could and did not determine it was more probable than not that petitioner wrote both letters.' So what we have here is another case were the prosecution suborned perjury and solicited perjury.

DISCUSSION

1.

THE INSTANT PETITION FOR WRIT OF HABEOUS CORPUS MUST BE GRANTED AS IT IS TIMELY AND SUPPORTED BY NEW EXCULPATORY EVIDENCE

Schulp v. Delo (1995) 130 L. Ed.2d 808 support this filing as timely since newly discovered evidence that is exculpatory in value was turned over in discovery by the Los Angeles District Attorney around May 2005, and this discovery was first given to appointed DNA attorney Mario DiSalvo, and petitioner was not aware of its discovery until attorney DiSalvo mailed him a copy of the DNA motion. Petitioner then filed in a timely manner after he diligently tried to gather other discovery in support of relief. The nonexistent delay was explained in the instant writ to wit the respondent seems to be oblivious. Petitioner could not file sooner as he could not have guessed in a million years that Thierry would send yet another confession, this time to the Attorney General. Swain & Gallego are moot; since good cause was shown, so there is no delay as petitioner timely filed, and the superior court opinion never said anything about timeliness.

The manifest need for collateral attacks on criminal judgments, however, must be tempered with the knowledge that mistakes in the criminal justice systems are sometimes made. Despite the substantive and procedural protections afforded those accused of committing crimes, the basic characters governing our society wisely hold open a final possibility for prisoners to prove their convictions were obtained unjustly. (U.S. Canst., art. 1 , §9, cl.2 [limiting federal government's power to suspend writ of habeas corpus].) A writ of habeas corpus may thus provide an avenue of relief to those unjustly incarcerated when the normal, [21 Cal.4th 704] method of relief--ie., direct appeal is inadequate" (In re Harris (1993) 5 Cal.4th 813,328, fn. omitted) , and the Great Writ has been justifiably lauded as '" the safe-guard and Palladium of our liberties'" (Clark, supra 5 Cal.4th. at p.764. quoting In re Bergarow (1901) 133 Cal.349, 353, 65 p.828i see also Lancher v. Thanas (1996) 517 U.S. 314, 322, 116 S.Ct. 1293, 134 L.Ed.2d 440, quoting Smith v. Bennet (1961) 365 U.S. 708, 712, 81. s.ce, 895, 6 L.Ed.2d 39 [writ of habeas corpus is the "highest safeguard of liberty"]). Robbins, supra, 1 8 Cal. 4th 770, [11] A claim or a part thereof that is substantially delayed nevertheless will be considered on the merits if the petitioner can demonstrate good cause for the delay A claim that is substantially delayed without good cause, and hence is untimely, nevertheless will be entertained on the merits if the petitioner demonstrates (i) that error of constitutional magnitude led to a trial that was so fundamentally unfair that absent the error no reasonable judge or jury would have convicted the petitioner; (ii) that the petitioner is actually innocent of the crime or crimes of which he or she was convicted. The petitioner has met all four of the Clark exceptions. The Discovery was made on May 20th, 2005 and petitioner on August 23rd, 2006 within 90 days of the Superior Court decision filed the instant petition. Its ironic that respondent quotes <u>In re Dixon</u> because evidence has disappeared and one major witness has died eg., In Thierry's confession on the Los Angeles District Attorney's letter head (Petitioner Ex 'e') it states the very first confession Thierry made "was destroyed and the record was erased." Also officer Douglas Skaggs(4) is now deceased. The destruction of evidence Denies petitioner due process and in the evidentiary hearing much will be revealed about these facts. <u>In re Hall</u> petitioner sought writ of habeas corpus following his conviction of first degree murder and related charges, and imposition of sentenceof life imprisonment. The Supreme Court, Mosk, J., held that: (1) newly discovered and credible evidence which undermines the entire case of the prosecution warranted habeas relief; (2) identification testimony was false evidence which also warranted habeas corpus relief; (3) record amply supported referee's finding that petitioner was denied constitutionally adequate representation (5. Douglas Skaggs was the first person Thierry Confessed to and Officer Skaggs made a taped dying confession about petitioner being falsely convicted. (see taped confession attached to Judicial Notice.) of counsel by his attorney's failure to adequately investigate the case and challenge identification procedures utilized by police. Writ granted; judgment of conviction vacated; case remanded.

It is obvious when the information offered in support of the claim was obtained as explained in the instant writ, it was turned over in discovery by the Los Angeles D.A. in response to petitioners DNA motion in May 1995, and it was impossible for him to know that the Attorney General or the D.A. and Police were withholding the confession by Thierry, obviously when petitioner was appointed counsel then the D.A. decides to turn it over before it was stumbled upon inadvertently.

There was no need for former counsel to make a declaration to the effect as it was turned over by the prosecution. (Petitioner Ex 'B' pg.2 DNA Motion) When When an evidentiary hearing is held Mr. DiSalvo will testify to the discovery.

Petitioner proffered more than the fact that "he is a layman at law and was rendered ineffective assistance of counsel and that the prosecution failed to turn over exculpatory evidence as required by law." The new exculpatory evidence negates all this rhetoric about delays, the respondent is obviously having a hard time figuring out and coping with how the D.A. and A.G. dropped the ball by thwarting petitioners due process and constitutional rights, by withholding critical newly discovered exculpatory evidence which clears petitioner of any involvement in this crime. It is obvious that petitioner met a significant burden of proof of his actual innocence, just based on the respondent being ordered to answer these allegations. This evidence is new and therefore was never presented at trial. The respondent gives an (RT#) as the support for his bogus claim that the jury has considered this new exculpatory evidence. This evidence along with all the other evidence of innocence cannot be related. In addition since the D.A. destroyed exculpatory biological DNA evidence which would have additionally proven him factually and actually innocent, then petitioner must be given the benefit of the doubt that this destroyed evidence would have bee caused the jury to find him not guilty. But now that this evidence was destroyed without notifying the petitioner of his right to request its salvage (P.C. 1417.2; 1417.5; 1417 9) the only reasonable and fair remedy is to grant petitioners petition and release him immediately.

The respondent argues that the Thierry letter has no date to say when it was written and no return address, and it doesn't indicate when it was mailed to the attorney general's office. Well the respondent has already stated that the date on the letter from Ms. Santos of the attorney general's office was dated "1983" which shows that at the latest is was nailed written and mailed 3 days before Ms. Santos wrote her letter to Thierry and the Los Angeles Police, considering the mail delivery. In addition they have the envelope to the letter that was never turned over in discovery, nor did the D.A. turn it over in 2005. SO the Los Angeles Police and the D.A. must have a record of they received the confession/w the Santos letter, and again they failed to turn over that information in discovery as well, it seems <u>Brady</u> violations keep mounting as time goes on.

The respondent fails to address this critical information. The respondent seems to call Legal Analyst Santos a liar stating she was in error by typing 1983 as the year on her letter. Also her letter states Thierry was notified that they received his letter and yet **Thierry never wrote back stating it wasn't him that authored the confession**, which he would have done if he never sent it. And Ms. Santos had to have Thierry's return address in order to notify Thierry they received his confession. So its a guarantee that petitioner never received that letter from Ms. Santos at this or any other time. When an evidentiary hearing is held this court will see the institutional legal mail logs to show that the attorney general never mailed petitioner anything. So respondents claims that petitioner fabricated this confession is next to impossible. In addition Thierry's CDC # and housing is in the confession which shows that he is incarcerated. Why is he in prison?

Petitioner attaches as exhibit 'A' a fax of Thierry's latest arrest record showing the crime for which he is currently incarcerated. Also as (Exhibit 'B') petitioner attaches a copy of his work schedule from Ernst Steam Cleaning which shows that the place of business where Thierry murdered the Jack In The Box Manager was in fact a client of petitioner which confirms Thierry's statement that he stole petitioners invoice from his truck. (Petitioner Ex 'B' Attachment 'A') Petitioner and Thierry are the same height, weight, they both ware hearing aids, they have the same first name (Roger) both of these crimes-occurred at client of petitioner and the 2nd one at the Jack in the Box was after petitioner was convicted and in fulfillment of Thierry's threat to do the crime again. (RT 652-653) The crimes were done exactly the same way, so all these matches are beyond coincidence but are in fact by Thierry's design. It is the respondent that is failing to read more into Thierry's confession, to wit the respondent has a moral obligation not to prosecute the innocent.

The respondent again tries to assert that this issue was argued at the trial and it is very impossible to have been argued at trial when the confession in question did not exist until 1993. For whatever reason

Thierry used the alias Crazy E/Roggie petitioner does not know. Maybe he was trying to escape detection and help petitioner after a guilty conscience. Thierry did turn himself in and confessed to the Los Angeles P .D.and we will ask Thierry about this at the evidentiary hearing.

(6. On exhibit 'B' see the date 5/03/80 Thursday.)

We have no idea if the jury considered the 'Roggie/Crazy E' letter in finding petitioner guilty, but we can and will subpoena them for the evidentiary hearing and ask them the reason they found petitioner guilty • The respondent is so afraid of the truth coming out despite good cause and due diligence being shown, he request that the instant petition be summarily denied and he ignores the fact that the Superior Court never suggest that and nor has this court, the evidence in petitioners favor is to strong and must not be swept under the rug by a summary denial, this petition must be granted in the interest of justice.

PETITIONER OBJECTS TO REPONDENTS DISCUSSION

(2.)AND PETITIONER CLAIMS THE INSTANT WRIT IS NOT A SUCCESIVE PETITION BECAUSE OF NEWLY DISCOVERED EXCULPATORY EVIDENCE

It is senseless and baseless for the respondent to recite cases about timeliness and successive petitions when it is clear petitioner has presented newly discovered exculpatory evidence. The newly discovered grounds were not known to petitioner at the time of any prior collateral attack on the judgment.

Clark.

Petitioner made no reference to previous state habeas cases because

He is arguing newly discovered evidence and has sufficiently proferred great justification for this writ. In re Clark the instant petition cannot be summarily denied for untimeliness nor for successive petition because it is clear the A.G. and Police withheld newly discovered exculpatory evidence (Petitioner., Ex 'B' Attachment 'A') <u>Schulp v. Delo (1995) 130 L. Ed.2d 808</u>; Any old grounds previously presented now become new grounds as they help corroborate the new evidence In re Williams John Clark (1993) Ca1.4th 750,855 P.2d 729; "The Supreme Court Baxter;J. held that • (2) Courts will consider successive delay petitions if there is error of constitutional magnitude leading to a fundamentally unfair trial, if the petitioner was actually innocent of the crime, or if the petitioner was convicted under an invalid statute; and (3) ... that there was a fundamental miscarriage of justice." The petitioner has shown that the facts upon which he relies were not known to him and could not have been discovered by him at any time substantially earlier than the time of his motion for DNA **....** " [Citations.] <u>Shipnan, supra</u> 62 Ca1.2d at p.230, 42 Cal. Rptr. 1, 399 P.2d 993; accord, <u>In re Clark</u> (1993) 5 Ca1.4th 750, 799, "The petitioner has been aver not only to the probative facts upon which the basic claims rest, but also he has detailed the time and circumstances under which the facts were discovered, in order for the court to be able to determine as a matter of law whether the litigant has proceeded with due diligence [.]"21 Cal. Rptr.2d 505; If the instant petition is delayed because of petitioner-nc)'E being able to state a prima facie case for relief on all the bases believed to exist , delay in seeking habeas relief may be justified when the petition is untimely filed if the petitioner can demonstrate that he had good reason to believe that other meritorious claims existed and the existence of those facts supporting those claims could not with due diligence have been confirmed at an earlier time; delay would not be justified unless petitioner demonstrates that there was good reason to believe that further investigation would lead to facts supportive of a clearly meritorious claim. This would be the case when petitioner filed the DNA. motion in which the respondent in discovery turned over newly discovered exculpatory evidence eg., "Thierry Confession." This warrants issuance of a writ of habeas corpus based on newly

156

discovered evidence, which completely undermines the prosecution's case, creates fundamental doubt in the accuracy of the proceedings and points unerringly to innocence.

This court must allow for these issues to play out in an evidentiary hearing, as it will be amazed at the totality of the miscarriage of justice done in this case. In re Clark, supra 5 Cal.4th at p.766, 21; People v. Gonzalez (1980) 51 Cal.3d 1179, 1246; In re Hall (1981) 30 Cal.3d 408, 417.

PETITIONER OBJECTS TO RESPONDENTS REQUEST THAT HABEOUS CORPUS MUST BE DENIED AND PETITIONER REQUESTS THAT MERITS BE MET AND PETITION GRANTED

Courts and commentators have Imposed on the prosecutor a constitutional duty to volunteer exculpatory evidence In U. 8. v. Agurs 427 U. 8.97, 103, 96 (1976) The American Bar Associations standards for Criminal Justice, specifically referred to in Giglio provides:

The prosecuting attorney's obligation under this section extends to material and information in this possession or control of members of his staff and of any others who have participated in the investigation or evaluation of the case and who either regularly reports or with reference to the particular case have reported to his office.

Concurred in: <u>Barbee v. Warden</u> 331 F.2d 842 (4th Cir. 1964); <u>U.8. v. Butler</u>,567 F .2d 885, 889 (9th Cir. 1978); <u>U.S. v. Morell</u>, 524 F. 2d 550, 555 (2nd Cir. 1975).In <u>Koch v. Puckett</u>, 907 F. 2d 524, 530-31 The police are also part of the prosecution, and the taint on the trial is no less if they rather than the States Attorney, were guilty of the non-disclosure. If the Police allow the State's Attorney to produce evidence pointing to guilt without informing him of other evidence in their possession which contradicts this inference 8tate Officers are practicing deception not only on the States Attorney but on the Court and defendants. (Petitioner. Ex. 'B' and "c") (RT 311)

(Petitioner., Ex.B [Ex.B (Attachment A)].) Recognizing withholding of exculpatory Evidence by Police is imputed to the prosecution. <u>Boone v. Pad</u> 541F. 2d 447-450-51 (4th Cir. 1976)

The petitioner meets the <u>Brady</u> test to a greater degree than <u>Brady </u>and it is likely that his case will become the controlling case over <u>Brady</u>. The reason petitioner meets test (i) is that: Favorable evidence was exculpatory and impeaching. The Thierry confession was received by theAttorney General in 1 993. (Petitioner. Ex. 'B' Attachment 'A') They failed to turn it over knowing that it was favorable to the petitioner. This confession give facts unknown to the jury which would undermine the respondents entire case, to wit no reasonable jury would have found petitioner guilty. The confession by Thierry states things like:

"I first came in contact with the falsely accused Mr. Roger Lee, on *5/4/80-:-* at Jack in the Box. (The Jack in the Box was a client of petitioner at which Thierry robbed, stabbed and killed the store manager.)

(Lines 7-10 of the Thierry confession.)

This is important because the jury never knew this and that Thierry worked at the Jack in the Box that was a client of petitioner, this is beyond coincidence, its by Thierry's design. (lines 12-13 of Thierry's Confession) Thierry also states:

"I saw a way to use Mr. Lee as a scapegoat for my crimes,

because of having the same name."

This is critical because the jury didn't know that someone with the same name claimed to have committed this these crimes. This is also beyond coincidence, it is by design, Thierry's design. Thierry also states on (lines 19-26) :

"I had a friend that worked there and I contacted him to see if he could tell me when the steam cleaners were coming back, he checked and said on September 10th, at midnight. So the 10th, came around and I went to MacDonalds. on Crenshaw, and I got there about 10: 30 p.m. I got my friend to steal the keys for me, so the steam cleaners couldn't do their job, and because I didn't want them around when I robbed the place that night."

This is important because the jury didn't know another suspect was was involved and this is also supported by the police report (PR 636) that shows there was an unidentified shoe print that had to belong to Thierry's

7. The date on exhibit 'B' is 5/3/80,

and Thierry appears to be off by one day, but the address is spot on. crime partner. Thierry then states: *(AS 8* lines 2-7)

"I went to the side door and knocked on the door, the victim came to the door and put her face up against the glass to try and see who was there, she said come closer so I can see who you are. It was pitch dark outside and I had brown shoe polish on my face, and all black clothes & shoes & gloves and a hat."

This is very critical and exculpatory as the jury never heard that Thierry came to the side from the victims own mouth, (PR 4 of 7) But the Police report said the side door and Thierry also says the side door, which Calls into question the victims recollection of events and her credibility. Its also important, because Thierry says she had to put her face up against the glass to see who was there. This supports the victims consistent struggle to 1.D. petitioner as assailant. (RT 646) (PR p. 18 lines 25-26) **" ... wasn't very light in there." "It was difficult for me to see."** (PL p.44, lines 5-6) **"Most of the time I had an oxygen mask over my face, and I couldn't see very well."** In (PR 9 of 13) the victim states: **"... This picture was not as blurry as the first one and even though I thought the first one looked like the person you arrested, I'm absolutely positive that the second picture was in fact the individual you should be looking for."**

(PL p. 54 , lines 14-17)(RT 362) " .. lighting that would be difficult." The fact that Thierry states that 'he had on all black clothes & gloves and brown shoe polish on his face, gives great support to the other confession Thierry gave to Los Angeles D.A. Investigator 'Walt Bure,' in which he states 'he put shoe polish on his face. (Petitioner. Ex. "C") These confessions were written years apart and like the Bible are very consistent and accurate. The respondent has long claimed petitioner fabricated that confession on the D.A.' s letter head. But this new confession helps put that theory to rest, since they are consistent and supportive of each other. One can only wonder what the other confession that was destroyed by the D.A. and for which the police evidence record was erased. (Petitioner. Ex8. As will stand for Roger Thierry's confession from this point forward., B I) When an evidentiary hearing is held these facts will come to greater light. In (AS p.2, lines 8-12) Thierry states:**"She opened the door and said are you from the steam cleaners? I didn't answer, and then she said 'what's your name,' I said**

162

**my name is Roger and I want a job
because I got fired for bringing these
keys to you."**

This is critical and exculpatory because
Thierry confirms that the victim didn't know
the petitioners name nor Thierry's name as
the victim stated she did. (PR 5 of 7) And
she didn't know if the person worked for the
steam cleaners, she just assumed he did. The
jury did not get to hear these facts which
contradict the victims perjured testimony. In
addition the petitioner didn't lose his job
because keys to victim. Petitioner was self-
employed and a sub-contractor.

In (AS p. 2, lines 12-16) Thierry states:

**"I handed her the keys then
pulled out a screwdriver
and she ran to the office."**

The jury heard the victim testify that the
suspect handed the keys to her, but in the
police report; she states he pushed them into
her pocket. (PR 4 of 7) The jury never heard
that the suspect came with a screwdriver, in
which we will see is very significant and
exculpatory. Thierry continues:

**"I trapped her and made her go
to the safe and open it.
As she was opening the safe I
saw a small knife on the counter,
I grabbed it and put the**

screwdriver in my pocket."

This would explain to the jury how the victim survived, as we now Know the reason being is she was stabbed by a screwdriver. In (AS p.2 lines 16-17) Thierry states:

**"I took the money and we both
had to crawl back to the
office, so no one could see us."**

This would have been helpful for the jury as the prosecution gave Great weight to this event thinking that only the victim was made to crawl.(PL p.20) In (AS p.2, lines 18-20) Thierry states:

**"I turned the lights off, and she said I
please don't rape me, I said don't worry
lady I'm gay, she said 'oh good. '"**

This was important to the jury because the victim said the lights Stayed on, but if they were off that makes it impossible for the victim to identify suspect and other events. As well Thierry saying the victim asked not to be raped and that he was gay. The petitioner is far from being gay, and the victim failed to make this statement known. In (AS p.2, Lines 20-23)Thierry states:

**"I then took the knife I found
and cut her throat, she then**

**grabbed the knife blade and
broke it, when she did that, she
cut the palm of my hand trying
to fight me off. "**

The jury surely needed to know that Thierry didn't bring the knife to the crime which means that its not premeditated attempted murder, and the victim cut Thierry with the knife. This is truly crucial, critical and exculpatory facts because this is why petitioner filed for the DNA motion. As Thierry states the same facts in his other confession taken by D.A. investigator Walt Bure. (Petitioner. Ex. IC') It behooves petitioner that the respondent could blatantly withhold both confession knowing that -Thierry say, he was cut and that DNA wasn't available, but DNA did cane into effect after Thierry sent the 1993 confession to respondent, and the respondent had amoral obligation to turn these confession over and too preserve the exculpatory DNA evidence. The petitioner is positive that had DNA been available in 1980 the jury would have found him not guilty! Park v. Delo, (P.C. §1417.2; 1417.5 and 1417.9.) At the evidentiary hearing, Thierry will be called to show his knife wound on his hand. In (AS p.2, lines 23-24) Thierry states:

**"I then pulled out the
screwdriver and began to stab
her several times."**

This is important because the jury was lead to believe the victim was stabbed by the broken knife handle, but now we know it was a screwdriver which explains why most of her wounds were superficial. (RT437) and even D.A. investigator Walt Bure agrees. (Petitioner. Ex. 'C") In (AS p.2 lines 25-27) Thierry states:

"Plus I told her I wouldn't kill her, I told her I wouldn't be around to mop the floors anymore, because I used to help my friend."

Here the jury didn't get to hear that Thierry didn't try to kill the victim, which changes the degree of the charges of premeditated attempted murder, to just great bodily injury, attempted murder should not have been considered. Thierry also confirms that he used to mop the floors, just as the victim stated. (PR 4 of 5) The petitioners job was not to clean floors, surely the victim knew Thierry after all, and this will shall find out at the evidentiary hearing. In (AS p. 3, lines 1-2) Thierry states:

"I then left the office and let my friend inside to look around for about 20 minutes and then we left."

Again the jury didn't know about third person, which explains why there was a third shoe print in blood. (RT 642) Plus petitioners shoe didn't match the prints at the crime scene. Petitioner wears a size 9 inch shoe was more than 12' inches. (RT 638) We've got all this information that the jury and court never heard, because the respondent withheld this exculpatory evidence for 12 years knowing that petitioner claimed actual innocence depriving him of due process and discovery. The respondent raises an issue that petitioner must rebut. The jury never heard the fact that Thierry sent petitioner a letter while he was in the county jail. Petitioner's attorney did not use the letter as part of his strategy, and Mr. Peter M. Jones will be called to testify to this effect at the evidentiary hearing. Mr. Jones has failed to respond to petitioners request for this specific work product and request for declaration to this effect, but he will respond to a subpoena. The questioned document examiner Geoff Collins' testimony is not reliable as he took liberty to embellish his testimony in regards to those letters. (RT 520) In the confession taken by D.A. investigator Walt Bure, Thierry states that he goes by the name Roger. (Petitioner. Ex. 'e') If the jury could have seen these confessions and heard from Walt Bure that Thierry confessed to him face to face than surely they would have found petitioner not guilty. The respondent asserts that because Thierry/Roger/Crazy E, makes no mention of being with petitioner in county jail, that the Thierry confession is suspect. Well maybe respondent would like to make a wish for a more detailed confession, and his wish will come true when Thierry is called to testify at the evidentiary hearing. And surely the respondent doesn't think Thierry had access to the trial transcript of this courts opinion in case Number F105836. The details that Thierry provides goes far beyond what was ever known in this case.

It is strange and convenient that respondent did not interview Ms. Gloria Santos to see when and how she came in contact with the Thierry confession, and on what date, and to what return address she notified Thierry of the status of his letter. For all we know there was a cover letter from Thierry? Ms. Santos had to have an envelope with Thierry's return address, but once again this piece of exculpatory evidence must have been conveniently destroyed, as it most definitely was never turned over in discovery to this very day. The confession is clearly written and signed by Thierry, under the penalty of perjury, so that explains who wrote it, and at the evidentiary hearing Thierry will testify to all the respondents inaccurate speculations and prove him them false and baseless. If petitioners trial counsel had either one of the Thierry confessions it would have been a simple task of convincing the jury that Thierry is Roggie/Crazy E and that he wrote the aforementioned letters and confessions. As noted Thierry identified himself as Roger, so it is without question that the jury would have known that Thierry is Roggie/Crazy E, and that he was in the county jail with petitioner in a different Pod, and that Detective Stokes came to see petitioner in the jail and handed petitioner the 'Roggie' letter and envelope and asked petitioner if he wrote it to which he said NO! So this is why petitioner only had one thumb print on the right margin/middle side of the letter, so its no mystery that petitioners print is on the letter. Even so it doesn't place petitioner at the scene of the crime. This Court has to see the following is beyond coincidence and must be by design:

(1) Both petitioner and Thierry have the same first name, which is why the victim named petitioner.

(2) Wrote letters as Roggie/Crazy E, saying he would do this crime again, (RT 652-653) He did do it again in exactly the same way and this time he killed the store manager, a black woman, and if the prosecution had charged him when he first came to confess that victim would still be alive!

(3) The Jack in the box in Los Angeles, CA

is the place of the second Thierry attack as promised, and this restaurant was a client of the petitioner, which confirms that this is the place where Thierry went into the petitioner's truck and took his invoice and decided to use petitioner as a scapegoat for his crimes.

(4) Thierry and petitioner both ware hearing aids on both ears, And the victim forgot this major detail, which helps proves she didn't get a good look at suspect. If she had seen petitioner 3 times before surely she would know that petitioner wears hearing aids.

(5) Both Thierry and petitioner are the same height and weight.

(6) Both victims had their throats cut and money was taken.

This is BEYOND COINCIDENCE, ITS BY DESIGN! THIERRY'S DESIGN!!!

The court should know that Thierry Confessed on a local T.V. show In Sacramento, CA called the Armstrong & Getty Show, back in 2002.

Thierry first confessed to Los Angeles Police officer Douglas Skaggs, in 1980. As a result officer Skaggs taped a confession of himself stating in summary, 'that Thierry came to him and confessed, and that D.A. Roland

LeBlanc chose not to do anything about it because Thierry is white and petitioner is black. I Officer Skaggs also noted had in his possession petitioners shoe, which to then had been determined to have no blood on them. (Petitioner. Ex. IB' Attachment 'B') Officer Skaggs has since died.

However, petitioner is providing this court and respondent with a copy of the taped confession and a certified copy of the transcribed confession. It would have been nice if officer Skaggs had revealed this information before he died, but it is what it is, a fact!

A. THE DISTRICT ATTORNEY HAD GOOD MOTIVE TO DESTROY EXCULPATORY BIOLOGICAL EVIDENCE BECAUSE IT WAS HIS BLOOD

This court will see that its not beyond the realms of possibility that District Attorney, Roland LeBlanc planted blood evidence .on petitioners shoe. Trial counsel recognized how unusual it was that the shoes had been examined by and experienced expert who failed to find any trace of blood on the shoes until some unknown person spotted what looked like a trace amount of blood and the shoes were reexamined. (RT 695-696) Such an unusual occurrence apparently alerted counsel to the extract testimony as to who had pointed out such a very small stain to the expert who had already examined them. The only clue contained in the record as to who that Person was may have been is provided in the Physical Examination Report dated 12-19-80, (Petitioner. Ex 'B' Attachment I B') (See foot 5 for Skaggs Confession) which states prosecuting Deputy District Attorney, Roland LeBlanc, was the person who requested that the shoes be re-examined. This is perfect since the D.A. know there is no such thing as DNA testing to prove its his blood, so he thinks, 'Why not prick my finger or pick a scab and put a spot of blood on the shoe, my case is weak so this will convict him for sure." And since the expert examiner Ms. Bush, testified that the reason she re-examined the shoes was because it was pointed out to her that there was a very small blood stain on the sole of the shoe, we are left to with the reasonable conclusion that the person who pointed that out this was Mr. LeBlanc. (RT 625) There is no evidence suggesting that someone had pointed out this very small stain to Mr. LeBlanc, which then leads us to the logical conclusion that it was Mr. LeBlanc who found (planted) and pointed out that very small stain to Ms. Bush. However, there is nothing in the record to show that Mr. LeBlanc ever had possession of the shoes. But thank God for officer Skaggs who places the shoes in Mr. LeBlanc' hands. (see fn. 5) So conveniently for the prosecution, not knowing about officer Skaggs confession, under unclear circumstances some unknown person finds, on a greasy unwashed shoe, one very small stain. (RT 639) This fact in itself moves the possibility of the evidence having been tampered with beyond the realm of bare speculation. Considering this was the only physical piece of evidence to support the prosecutions case, it would concern Mr. LeBlanc that By 1996 DNA testing would have proved that it was his blood on the shoe, so why not have the evidence destroyed before petitioner finds out he can get the shoe tested and on top of that I won't notify him that he has a right to request that the biological evidence be preserved. (P.C. §1417.2; 1417 • 5 & 1417.9.) The prosecution did withhold exculpatory evidence and destroy biological evidence and this petition must be granted. (Brady v. Maryland(1963) 373 U.S. 83

B. THE PROSECUTOR DID IN FACT KNOWINGLY ELICIT FALSE TESTIMONY FROM THE VICTIM AND PETITIONER IS ENTITLED TO HAVE HIS WRIT GRANTED AND TO BE RELEASED FROM CUSTODY

The petitioner objects to respondents claims that prosecutor Robert LeBlanc never

173

suborned or solicited perjury from the victim Rita Daniels. We've already seen how inconsistent the victims testimony was, but let us take it a little further and learn of more instances in which the victim perjured herself and how this leads up to the prosecutor soliciting and suborning perjury. The petitioner contends that the procedure used by the police for the initial identification of the suspect by the victim/eyewitness in the instant case was improperly suggestive, as was the subsequent in-court identification of petitioner by the victim/eyewitness.

The record reflects that on September 25, 1980, two Polaroid photographs were taken of petitioner by an I. Bureau Technician. (RT 586) These two photos were taken to the hospital by Detective Stokes and shown to the victim, who at the time was recovering from surgery in the intensive care unit. (RT 586-587) At the time, Detective Stokes believed the victim was going to survive the assault. (PR 7 of 13) According to the physician on duty in the emergency room, the victim was in stable condition when she arrived at the hospital. (RT 430) According to the discharging physician, the victim had just gotten out of surgery when Detective Stokes showed her the photos. (cr 42; RT 365) And the victim would have been able to return to work after a couple of weeks.(RT 439). While in surgery she had been administered a general anesthetic. (cr 54) She had lost consciousness while in surgery. (RT 372) There were no other photos taken or shown to victim by detective Stokes. (RT 366, 598) Detective Stokes was familiar with the term "photo Lineup." (RT 598) Yet Detective Stokes admitted to not having used the procedure of showing a six photo lineup to show the victim. (RT 599) Detective Stokes testified that the victim did not have her glasses on at any time during this identification process, and that she asked her daughter to obtain the eyeglasses and bring her a pair. (RT 599) The victim testified that she had put her glasses on to look at the photos. (CI' 55) The victim testified she needed to wear her glasses in order to see to write. (RT 364) The victim testified that without her glasses she'd have difficulty identifying the suspect. (RT 367) The victim testified that when talking to Police Officers at the hospital, she was wearing an oxygen mask. (RT 358) The oxygen mask made it difficult for her to see very well. (IT 44) She doesn't remember the faces of the investigating officers who interviewed her at the hospital mask because of the oxygen mask. (cr 54) Detective Stokes testified that the victim appeared to be in a lot of pain. (RT 599) Detective Stokes testified that the victim was breathing very heavily, that she was hooked up to a chest tube, her neck was in a brace, and her hands were shaking. (RT 603) Detective Stokes testified that her hands were shaking so much, he had to hold the photos in order for her to be able to see them. (RT 604) While there is obviously no reason to doubt that the victim wasconvinced that she knew who had attacked her, this does not necessarily mean that she was correct. It was around 3:00 a.m., she was alone and working later than usual, so she was probably tired. (RT 294; PR 3 of 5) She was working in the office doing paperwork when she heard a knock at the door. (RT 293-294) She required glasses in order to do the paperwork she was involved with.

(RT 322) It was dark outside except for the lights in the parking lot, which were behind the suspect. (RT 298,299) The lights inside had been dimmed considerably. (RT 349) The people who do the cleaning show up during these hours. (RT 347) They were due to comeback any day. (RT 350) She went to see who was at the door, and saw someone standing there holding up a set of keys which looked to be the ones that had turned up missing about a month earlier. (RT 294) She assumed the person was there to clean the floors. (PR 8 of 1 3) She opened the door and the person with the keys told her he had been fired. (RT 300) Now at that point, she had no reason not to believe what she had been told by the person. After all, she had seen Roger around the restaurant before, and knew he was a young black man. She talked to Roger's employerabout the missing keys, and she and the employer had come to the conclusion that Roger had taken the keys even though there was no evidence to support that conclusion. She knew his first name. However, she was worried about what Roger might do if he found out that she was responsible for getting him fired. She had no reason to expect Roger to show up, except to do some wrong. (PR 4 of 7) In light of all this, some substantial questions come to mind. Why would she open the door for someone she believed she had reason to fear? Why did she ask his name if she knew him and recognized him? Was she wearing her glasses at the time? Why did she think he was there to clean the place since she believed she was responsible for getting him fired from working at the restaurant? The most reasonable conclusion is that she did not recognize the person as Roger; in fact, she thought it was someone else at first; someone from the cleaning company who was there to work, and had brought back themissing keys. It was only after hearing this "young black man"? say he had been fired, and his name was Roger, that she reached the conclusion that this was the man whom she feared would do her harm if he found out she had been responsible for getting him fired. This assumption was further supported by him telling her that he had come for compensation and the sudden appearance of a knife in his hand. (RT 301)

In hear, she ran toward the office for protection. (RT 301) She was followed by the **man,** who stopped her from gaining access to the office and closing the door (RT 301-302) With the knife in his hand, he told her to open the safe. (RT 302-303) At that point, it would be reasonable to assume that she was terrified, and convinced that this was the same man who she was afraid of. However, the keys the man had held up at the door had never been proven to have been taken from the restaurant by petitioner. (RT 355,414) In fact, the keys which disappeared about a month before the incident, were accessible to any number of people, who could have known that the victim blamed petitioner for their disappearance. (RT 350-352) Consequently, any number of young black males may have had access to both the keys and that information eg., (Thierry made himself up to look black by putting brown shoe polish on his face. Petitioner. Ex. 'B' [Ex. 'C') It is not entirely unreasonable to presume that Thierry, made up the look black could have gone to the restaurant and showed the victim the keys, told her name was Roger in order to mislead her, and easily place the blame on someone she already strongly suspected. Had Detective Stokes Provided the victim with more photos of different black men, or had a proper lineup been done, it may well have turned out that she would have been unable to pick out a suspect or possibly would have picked someone else altogether, especially considering the condition she was in when asked to identify the suspect. Additionally, the victim was white, the factor of cross racial identification was present in the instant case. There was never any other description of the suspect other than "young black man" (PR 8,9 of 13) There was no attempt made by Police to gather any further description from the victim before showing her the photos of the person she already believed was responsible. Petitioner contends that these facts establish conclusively that a reasonable probability has been demonstrated that the results of a proper photographic lineup could have at least provided some doubt in the victims mind of the identification of the suspect and/ or the jurors as well. There also exist by extension the reasonable probability that the identification of the suspect may have been regarded with sane mistrust by the police, who presumably then would have gone forward in their investigation of other possible suspects ie., (Thierry) such as anyone else who may have recently been fired or had problems in the past with the victim. Clearly, the procedure utilized by the police for the purpose of pretrial identification was unfairly suggestive, as well as entirely unreliable and thus deprived petitioner of his Constitutional guarantee of due process. It is the likelihood of misidentification which violates a defendant's right to due process. And defendant/petitioner here contends that not only was the confrontation procedure unfairly suggestive, but also under the totality of the circumstances, the identification was not reliable. (See <u>Neil v. Biggers</u> (1972) 409 U.S. 188, 93 S. Ct. 375, 34 L. Ed.2d 401) The factors to be considered in evaluating the likelihood of misidentification include "the opportunity of the witness to view the criminal at the time of the crime, the witness' degree of attention, the accuracy of the witness' prior description of the criminal, the level of certainty demonstrated by the witness at the confrontation." (<u>Neil v. Biggers, supra,</u> 93 S. ct. 375 at p. 382.) The witness testified that she had been wearing her glasses during the attack. (RT 322) The witness testified that she had been wearing her glasses while viewing said photographs. (RT 599; PR 9 of 13) The witness' recollection and testimony may be regarded as suspect in light of such contradictory testimony. Furthermore, the witness' glasses appeared in a photograph taken of the crime scene which showed them situated in blood, lying on the desk in the office where the attack took place. (RT 321) This cast further doubt as to the reliability of the witness' testimony of whether she had been wearing her glasses at during the attack, since the presence of blood on the desk demonstrate that the glasses could have become covered with blood on the desk or while on the desk during the attack. (cr 29 "I had to clean my glasses off because they were all bloody. And then I wrote a note.") The witness clearly took her glasses off after writing a note and left them on her desk. Under the circumstances, this presents a strong indication that the witness had a reflective habit of taking off her glasses when leaving her desk, and further raises a reasonable doubt as to whether or not she was wearing them at the time of the attack. To the extent that it is unknown whether the victim was wearing her glasses at the time of the crime, it is uncertain as to what degree of opportunity was afforded the viewing of the suspect by the witness during that time. While trial counsel failed to establish for the record the exact nature of her sight disability, it is Clear that she needed her glasses to do her work in the office. (Petitioner. Ex 'B' [Ex. 'D' Board of Prison Hearing Transcript p. 55 lines 15-16) The victim states "she didn't have her glasses on when viewing the photos of petitioner." This confirms perjury by the victim and solicitation and subordination by the prosecution even though this was already done by the police report and trail transcript. This contradictory and perjury proving statement by the victim is highly exculpatory and could not have been obtained by any other means. If this had been heard by the jury, it would have resulted in an acquittal. Additionally the lighting was very low in the area of the safe, which was close to the floor, making it difficult for the victim to exactly what the suspect was doing while the suspect was squatting down taking the money from the safe. (RT 362-363) The witness testified that she had been laying flat on the floor on her stomach during the time the suspect was taking the money from the safe. (RT 338) There was one light on in the office, and it wasn't very bright. (RT 307) This light was underneath some cupboards above the desk. (cr 49) During the time in the office the witness was being stabbed from behind while she was on her hands and knees, indicating that she had no real opportunity to view the suspect at that time. (RT 308) The witness testified that she got a good look at the suspect after he stopped stabbing her, when she turned around to tell him he could stop stabbing her and go, because he was standing right in the light of the office door for thirty seconds to a minute. (RT 364-365) This testimony was in direct contradiction to her earlier testimony that he was still stabbing her when she said that to him. (RT 310) Although the witness testified that she could see the suspect through her glasses unimpaired in spite of the blood running down them, she found it necessary to clean and put on her glasses before writing the note after the attack. (cr

29; RT 311, 364-365) The victim was unable to testify as to what kind of clothing was worn by the suspect, what color they were, if the suspect had been wearing gloves, or if the suspect had any facial hair. (RT 355-356) In fact, the only thing the witness was able to say about the physical appearance of the suspect was that the suspect was a "young black, male." This does not evince facts that the witness was very observant of anything in particular about the suspect which was most; likely due to the facts that she assumed it must have been petitioner after she saw what appeared to be the missing keys, the suspect told her his name was "Roger ;" she became frightened, was subsequently under a great deal of stress, and had already made up her mind about who the suspect was. Furthermore, the witness was unable to say exactly when or how the telephone was taken from the office, (RT 312) nor was she able to say how the broken knife handle got on the desk. (cr 28) The witness' prior physical description of the suspect was limited to "young, black, male." This description did nothing to distinguish the suspect from millions of other individuals, and therefore supported nothing beyond that description by which a reasonable identification of the suspect may have been made. While such a limited description was worthless for the purpose of identifying any suspect, it was very probative as to the level of attention given to the appearance of the suspect by the witness. As the witness had just come from surgery prior to viewing the photos, and because of the level of injuries sustained by the witness, it was reasonable to assume that she was under the influence of at least one powerful medication. That in itself should have been enough to cast substantial doubt on the reliability of the identification, but here we had the additional factors that she was not wearing her glasses, and the cross-racial nature of the identification. That the witness was able to identify the suspect with certainty from the profile photograph, in the condition she was in, apparently without her eyeglasses, should have given counsel for pause. (PR 9 of 13)Considering her lack of attention to the appearance of the suspect during the initial contact the night of the crime, and to her subsequent assumptions made at the time of the crime as to the identity of the suspect, a reasonable probability existed that had the victim been shown other photographs of different individuals, the outcome of her identification could have been much different.

Under the totality of the circumstances, the unreliability of the pretrial identification of the suspect would have been obvious by trial counsel's complete and thorough inquiry into all circumstances to prove

184

invalidity. Trial counsel was in an excellent position to make a prima facie case that the identification procedures fell short of the required due process. Trial Counsel knew of the critical nature of the identification, yet he did nothing pre-trial to test it's reliability. Trial Counsel should have made an attempt to force the burden of proof onto the prosecution. The prosecution would then have had to show that he in-court identification had an independent source or origin by clear and convincing evidence. Considering that practically the whole case of the prosecution rested on the eyewitness identification issue, there could have no rational trial tactic for the failure of the trial attorney to put the issue to a meaningful adversarial test. There is nothing in the record indicating that any other pre-trial identification was sought. During the in-court identification, the witness identified the suspect by stating "He's sitting next to the defense attorney." (RT 295) The witness knew who was on trial, she knew the defendant would be the person sitting next to the defense attorney. At the time she was asked to identify the suspect in court, she only had to make an assumption, not any reliable identification. Both the pre-trial and in-court confrontations virtually inevitable. Accordingly, trial counsel should have made a motion to suppress the tainted identification, as well as objection to the subsequent in-court identification, but failed to do so. (RT 295) Said failure to object waived the issue on appeal and forces petitioner now to raise it by way of the instant petition along with the prosecutorial misconduct and his role in the destruction of exculpatory evidence the destruction of biological evidence and solicitation of perjured testimony. Nowhere in the record does it indicate any reason for not following standard police procedure and utilizing a photographic lineup. Nowhere in the record is it indicated that the victim was in any danger of not surviving the attack after his initial interview with the victim. (PR p. 13 of 13) Her condition was "stable yet critical" as stated by detective Stokes. Detective Stokes had told petitioner that he understood the victim was in serious condition but that she was apparently going to survive the attack. (PR p. 7 of 13) If the victim was in such danger of death as to allow the unfairly suggestive and unreliable identification procedure utilized by Detective Stokes, then there was no reason for him to wait so long after he had the suspect in custody to take the pictures and show them to the victim. And if there was no great need for speed in the identification process, then there was no need to take the photos and show them to the victim at a time when the victim was obviously in no condition to reliably identify any such photos. She had just gotten out of surgery, where she had been administered general anesthesia and was undoubtedly under the influence of some pain medications, such as morphine, or some other powerful narcotic. Her vision was blurry enough to require her to wear her glasses when she wrote the note indicating who attacked her, yet Detective Stokes testified that she did not have her glasses available at the time she was asked to make an identification. She was in a great deal of pain, and had an oxygen mask partially blocking her vision. Her hands were shaking so badly she could not hold the photos still enough to look at them. And yet, here was a police officer asking her "Is this the guy?" while showing her only two photos of the person she was already convinced was responsible, If everyone was so sure of who the responsible party was, and that the victim would have been able to identify him, then there was no reason not to follow the standard police procedure utilizing a photographic lineup and therefore insure there was no question of unfair suggestibility or reliability. because the petitioner's case rested entirely on one eyewitness, and the petitioner contends that but for the unprofessional errors of both trial counsel and the prosecution, the outcome of the proceedings may have been more favorable to petitioner. What this court has just read was a detailed example of the massive and gross amount of perjured statements by the victim/witness and out right lies. When put in its proper context it is overwhelmingly egregious, and the prosecution had a duty not to allow the victim to make their perjured statements. He knew the police report showed that Detective stokes verified the victim never had her glasses on while trying to identify the petitioner, and yet he allowed her to testify that she did have her glasses on in both the preliminary hearing and trial. And the Coupe De Grace, is that at the petitioners Parole Hearing the victim finally after 15 years admits that she wasn't wearing her glasses. This critical exculpatory evidence was could not be obtained by any amount of due diligence, It has even prompted the Board of Prison Hearing to investigate this issue. There is no Identification and this matter should have never went to trial. The prosecution should have never let the victim give perjured testimony and he never should have with held the Thierry confessions. The jury was entitled to know the victim lied and committed perjury and call into question her credibility. The victim violated P.c. §118 and should have been found in contempt. The prosecution is guilty of solicitation and subornation of perjury pursuant. P.C. §966; P.C. §653f; and P .C. 127. He had a duty to correct evidence he knew to be false. Napuev. Illinois, 360 U.S. 264, 269 (1959); Mooney v. Holohan, 294,

U.S.103,112 (1935); <u>U. S. v. Young,</u> 17 F. 3d 12-1, 1203-05 (9th Cir. 1994) This is reversible error because the prosecutor knew the witness did not have her glasses on when viewing photos of petitioner. <u>U.S. v. Wallech,</u> 935 F.2d 445, 457

(2d

A. **BECAUSE THE PROSECUTION DID IN FACT DESTROY POTENTIALLY EXCULPATORY EXIDENCE THE PETITIONER IS ENTITLED TO BE RELEASED FROM '**

The respondent seems to be arguing for petitioner release, by citing the same cases and points therein. Petitioner without a doubt has went above and beyond to meet the two part test in <u>California v. Tranbetta,</u> (1984) 467 U.S. 497, 498.) (i) The evidence had exculpatory value that was apparent before the evidence was destroyed or lost ... , The petitioner should have been notified of the request to destroy this biological evidence. (See Ground 3. Petitioner. Ex. 'B' 6-7) Thierry states in both confessions that the victim cut his hand with the blade, this is great reason to preserve this evidence especially when respondent withheld both confessions and according to D.A. Investigator Walt Bure, he destroyed another confession. (Petitioner. Ex 'B' [Ex. "C"}) it should be noted that when Thierry is called to testify at the evidentiary hearing he will explain that when he turned himself in to the Los Angeles P .D., he confessed to the crime that petitioner is now incarcerated for and to the murder at Jack in the Box but he recanted before he was read his rights, believing he would get the Death Penalty for both crimes. At the evidentiary hearing Los Angeles police Detective, Russ Curry, who was the lead investigator in the Jack in the Box murder in the Thierry case, will be called to testify about these facts. The evidence should have been returned to the party to whom it belongs prior to final determination. P.C. §1417.2; 1417.5; P .c. §1417. 9., (2) The nature of the evidence is such that the defendant would be unable to obtain comparable evidence by other reasonably available means. The respondent has to be kidding if he thinks this evidence could be retrieved by any other means, and it seems to be beyond coincidence that the blood evidence was destroyed in 1996 when petitioner filed a claim of prosecutorial misconduct with the State Bar of California. Surely the D.A. Robert LeBlanc did not want test to show that it was his blood on the shoe which previously determined not to have blood on them. If Thierry says he was cut that means his blood was at the crime scene. The petitioner has tried to adjudicate the matter in the State Courts over the last 16 years. The respondent even cites the case numbers and ask for judicial review. How can he say The case was closed? Therefore, the Los Angeles Police Department would have no reason to investigate. Whether the Police had an obligation to investigate or not the petitioner was not given the right to preserve it and the only remedy is to release the petitioner immediately. There was no DNA testing in 1980, and so when DNA became available, it should have been tested, if it had the petitioner would have been exonerated years, ago. Thank God for the Thierry Confession and the taped confession from officer Douglas Skaggs.

Therefore, for the reasons discussed, respondent; submits that, because the prosecution **did** destroy exculpatory evidence and he did suborn and solicit perjury from the victim, and the Thierry confession is new evidence and the instant writ must be granted.

CONCLUSION

The petitioner pleads with this court to let the issues play out as a great injustice has been done. Pursuant to Rule 4.551 (c) [Order to Show Cause] (1) The court must issue an Order to Show Cause if the petitioner has made a prima facie showing that he is entitled to relief. In doing so the court takes petitioner's factual allegations as true and makes a preliminary assessment regarding whether, he petitioner would be entitled to relief if his or her factual allegations were proved. If so the court must issue an order to show cause. Petitioner request appointment of counsel on order to show cause, in this actual innocence case.

Respectfully submitted,

Roger Jason Lee, In Proper

Detective Ford:

Detective Ford was the arresting officer. He had been at the scene and had gathered up evidence and photos.

He had also called Rogers' boss, Joe Ernst, to inform him of the crime and to ask if he knew where

Roger lived. Mr. Ernst, stated that he didn't know the address but that it was a nice apartment off of Topanga and Victory. Roger had been home with his wife Mary. He and his wife were planning a trip to the zoo, when Joe Ernst called.

Mary answered and gave the phone to Roger.

"Roger where did you work last night?"

"I attempted to go to the Santa Barbara California account, but I got lost and turned around and came home."

"Roger will you come into the office and turn in you invoices?"

"But Mr. Ernst, what is this about? The invoices aren't due until next Monday,."

(It was Tuesday, the day of the crime).

Joe told Roger that someone robbed a McDonalds restaurant and stabbed the manager Rita Daniels and she said that it was you.

"There is no way that could be true. I was not there."

193

"Well Detective Ford will be here he wants you to meet him. "

Roger said ok and hung up.

Mary asked if all was well. Roger told her no it is not good.

"A customer was stabbed and robbed and said that I did it."

Mary asked. "What will you do?"

" I will go down there and clear this up and I'll be back to take you to the zoo."

Roger went to the office, spoke to Joe's wife and she said, the police will be here just have a seat.

Soon Detective Ford came in with a uniformed officer. He told Roger to stand up and put his hands behind his back.

"What are you doing I came to talk.

Detective Ford said, "we will talk downtown."

Rogers rights were never read to him, but it didn't matter because he would talk freely as he had nothing to hide. Although Roger did have a previous conviction for robbery and he didn't want them to try and pen this on him because of his prior, so he lied about being home all night, and never told Detective Ford, that he had tried to go to work that morning at midnight. Roger pleaded with him, saying he had no reason to do such a thing as he had a good job, and so did his wife and sister in law Paula Jordan.

Roger kept begging the Detective to take him to the hospital so the victim could see him and she would not be able to I.D. him. Detective Ford said,

"I can't do that but I will take pictures of you and have her look at them."

He took two polaroids and left Roger waiting in the interrogation room.

Roger sat there crying and stressed as he prayed for the victim and for this nightmare to be over. He just wanted to go home and take his wife to the zoo and forget about this terrible mistake.

An Hour later Detective Ford came back and said she identified you, she had trouble at first because she wasn't wearing her glasses. We sent her daughter to get them but we could not wait for her.

(There were no glasses to get because they had been booked into evidence) So we showed her the photos and she said I need my glasses to see. Ford said well this is the guy you said did this to you but we need a positive I.D. At first she said no that's not him. Then I said look again, look again.

She said, well it looks like him. Ford said are you

sure, are you positive. She said I think so. I said are you sure. She said well not on the profile but the front view I'm positive.

(It should be noted that during the preliminary hearing and the trial the victim Rita Daniels stated that she had her glasses on to look at the photos of Roger. Glasses that Detective Ford, testified were not available because they had been booked into evidence. Also Rita Daniels 15 years later testified at Rogers second parole hearing and said that she did not have her glasses on at the time. She was far sighted at the time and got a good look at the photos. Rita Daniels also testified at trial that when asked to I.D. the officers that showed her the photos, she said ("I can't because I was under heavy sedation, and I had tubes in and out of my body").

Detective Ford said he was going to have a mug shot

taken of Roger, and have him taken to the hospital for blood test to see if he was on drugs or if he had been drinking, and then I'll have you taken back to your truck. But after Roger was done giving a blood sample he was taken to L.A. County Jail never to be free still 21 year later.

Rita Daniels:

Rita Daniels, was a woman about 55 years old at the time of the brutal attack on her. She claims to have seen Roger on 2 or 3 occasions before when Roger service the exhaust system there before. The Rogers work schedule reflects that he had serviced that McDonalds 2 before over a 7 month period and one of those time Ms. Daniels was not present. As for the one time she was there was minimal contact totaling 2 minutes, long enough to ask for the roof hatch keys and then sing the invoice when the work was done.

Roger could not even I.D. her, she were put in a line-up. Ms. Daniels claims That on the 2 weeks prior to the robbery, when Roger last serviced the restaurant that her keys to the cabinets and the roof hatch came up missing that it was Roger or one of his workers that took the keys. There was no need for Roger to take the keys as he had been given a master key for all the roof hatches at all the McDonalds in California, so that he would not have to ask the managers for the keys. However she then tells her supervisor, Malik Barak, to contact the. Steam Cleaners office to see who took the keys. Joe Ernst called Roger to ask him if he had the keys, to wit he said no I did not need them I have the master key you gave me. So Roger thought that was the end of that until the night of the crime that changed his life and the life of his family as well as the Life of Ms. Daniels and her family forever!

Ms. Daniels, may be a sweet old lady but either her memory is bad or she lies like a rug. And as we shall see it is the later. She gave a statement and testified that she could identify the knife because she was not looking for evidence at the time. She said she could not identify the clothes or the color of them, nor could she identify the shoes. She could not say if the suspect had facial hair or not or whether he was wearing a beenie or hat. But yet she can identify Roger with no problem. She stated that after the knife broke the assault stopped but then later tells Detective Ford that the assault continues with the handle of the knife.

Joe Ernst:

Roger met Joe Ernst through his cousin Tina, (not

real name) who sold life insurance for the funeral

home that Roger was working for at the time.

Roger met Joe and was hired on the spot.

He began to work that night. Roger loved his new

job! There was potential to make more

money than he had ever made in his life. This was a

means to pay his bills and provide for his family

and to even save some. The job took Roger all over

California, to wit he got to visit many cities he never

imagines he would see. He also got to eat many

different foods at the restaurants he serviced. Life

was good and thanks to Joe Ernst, Roger's life was

going to change for the better or so he thought.

Joe was called to testify against Roger. Roger knew

that Joe was turning on him. After Roger was

arrested, Rogers Mother tried to recover Rogers pay

for the past 3 months and Joe refused to

pay, and he told Rogers Mother that he had to testify against Roger because he did not want to lose his contracts with McDonalds. Joe, unfortunately lied about everything he was questioned about. For example, Joe states that he has had many problems with Roger and had to fire him several times. This makes no good business sense, why keep someone that is such a problem child. Roger was never fired not even once, he was counseled once about feeding his workers better meals and about making sure he did a better job on Chinese restaurants. He stated that after the keys came up missing that he would not assign Roger any McDonalds contracts. However Rogers invoices and work schedule proved in court that Joe was lying. Roger had been assigned and working the McDonalds contracts even up to the day of the crime. When Joe spoke to Roger about the keys he never mad mention of any other problem with Rogers work. In fact the day before the crime Joe complemented Roger for his good work and apologized that some of his money had not come in yet and he would front. him money if he needed it. Roger declined the loan, and why would he do this if he was in desperate need of money. Joe says he only would allow Roger to work 2 or 3 jobs a week, and this was a lie as Rogers work schedule proved in court. Everything seemed to be so difficult for Joe to answer, or he did not know or could not remember. He stated that he did not assign any jobs to Roger after the 11th of September, after he said he only assigned him 2 or 3 jobs a week. Then he says I can't say for sure if he did any jobs after the 11th. He says he spoke to Roger about the keys being missing on the 11th and then states he spoke to Roger the next day at 8:00 a.m., a web of lies that the jury found credible.

PAULA JORDAN

Was the sister in law of Roger, the sister of his wife, Mary. Detective Ford questioned Paula, at the police station and she told the Detective that she Roger and her sister Mary Watched a late night talk show at 11:00pm and then her sister went to sleep and then Roger followed her after the show around midnight. Paula started to get ready for bed, and noticed that Roger was dressed and ready for work. She was in her bedroom and noticed that headlights were shining in her window and assumed it was the lights from Rogers work truck. Paula stated that around 4:00 am, Mary woke her up and asked her if she wanted to go to breakfast with her and Roger. Paula said no because she had to go to work soon. But

Detective Ford put a spin on that when it came to trial stating that Paula, told him that she saw Roger get dressed in the kitchen. (This would not happen since Roger was married and would never dress in front of Paula, nor would he do it in the kitchen). Ford stated that Paula told him that when she saw the headlights, she got out of bed and looked out the window and saw Rogers truck backing out.

GEOFF COLLINS:

He wrote a report stating that the letters confessing to crime allegedly written by Roggie could not be connected to Roger, because the writing was too disguised. However, during trial Mr. Collins, testified that it was more likely than not that Roger wrote the letter. Surely this had an influence on the jury.

GEORGE:

He delivered the blood evidence to the Department of Justice lab at Haskell and Rinaldi. He does not recall if the evidence box was sealed when he picked it up from DOJ. The only time he knew that it was sealed was Oct.3rd. This is relevant because in trial the evidence box had been sitting in the court room over night and wide open. The chain of custody was broken at that point and evidence contaminated that should not have been used.

JANET BUSH:

She tested Roger's tennis shoes and claims that they were black and white. But they were not, they were gray on white or white with light gray stripes. She initially found not blood on any of Roger's clothes or shoes. Then after a second examination which was requested by the D.A. Ronald LeBlanc, because he saw what appeared to be blood on one of the shoes. Firstly, he should not have been examining evidence and how could he see blood that CSI could not find with luminal. She says it could possibly be blood. Then she says it tested positive for human blood. She stated that the stain may have not been there the first time she examined the shoes. She was not able to type the blood to match the victim or Roger. The trace amount of blood was so small that there was nothing left for the defense to test. She examined the shoe prints and there were 3 prints in the blood and two of them could not be identified. They say it does not belong to anyone from the police department, but, yet there was only one assailant. The print they tried to connect .to Roger was a size 13 and Roger wore a size 9 *1/2*.

BUSH:

He is the sister of Officer Janet Bush. He was one of
the first officers on the scene. He collected evidence
which was two blouses that he believed belonged to
the victim and a pair of paints. He also interviewed
the victim at the hospital. His statement says the
victim opened the safe and she gave Roger the
money. Well this contradicts the victim's statement
that she opened the safe and Roger took the money
out.

If I Did It?"

The letter I would write to the victim

Date April 7, 2000

To: Ms. Rita Daniels,
C/O District Attorney Ronald LeBlanc

Dear Ms. Daniels;

I pray that the District Attorney will locate you and give you this letter. I have so much to tell you and I want to start by saying I am so very sorry for what I have done to you and your family & friends! I know that you never imagined me saying that, but I want you to know that I have always felt sorry, I have always felt remorse. Please know that I'm doing this against the advice of counsel and family because we feel that the board will now consider this as manipulation or a ploy to be found suitable. But I don't care, its more important that you hear exactly the who, what, when, where, why and how these horrible things happened to you. So please allow me to explain my silence.

To make is simple my now ex-wife and me along with Roger Thierry, were involved in this horrible attack on you. My then wife was pregnant and after we committed the crime, Thierry threatened that if we got caught, we were not to tell on him or he would make sure that my wife went to prison and that our child would be born behind bars and be without both parents. I know this is no excuse. In hindsight, we should have known the risk, but we just could not go back and change it. I can release this burden and weight that's been so heavy on my heart from day one and more importantly try to give some closer and relief if that is at all possible after I did this heinous and horrible thing to you.

I took advantage of you and the trauma you suffered, in that I knew after you gave your statement to the police that you were not aware that my ex-wife was there or that Thierry was there and that you could not remember what we were wearing or exactly how other events occurred. I figured this was a way for me to possibly be cleared of something I was actually guilty of and save my family that I put in jeopardy. I thought I could use the facts that you didn't know to free myself and I know that this was wrong and I'm so very sorry! Please bare with me as I explain the methods behind my madness.

About a month before the keys came up missing, I met Thierry at a Jack In The Box in Inglewood, on 10th and Prairie. I was cleaning their exhaust system when Thierry approached me and asked me for a job. I told him that I was not hiring right

now, but that I would keep him in mind. He asked me where I was from, I said Los Angeles. He asked me if I serviced any McDonalds' s in Los Angeles? I said yes all of them. He said I have a friend that works at one on Adams, and he says they keep thousands in the safe. I know this but what is your point? He said, "well my friend says it would be so easy to take the money out of there because the manager keeps the safe keys with other keys that they always give you guys to open the roof hatch. And all you'd have to do is take those keys and open the safe because they leave you alone sometimes, or when the manager is not looking you can open the safe and take the money without them knowing. I said why would you think that I would care about this. He said cause everybody wants easy money, and they would have to blame the manager for the missing money. I said why haven't you done this already. He said, I don't have a reason to have access to the keys. My friend that works there told me that the manager always gives the keys to the stem cleaners."
I said
"Well I'm not interested, thanks anyway."
He said,
"ok then your loss."
I went back to work and when done I left and saw no more of him. The next day I noticed that my work schedules were missing, I look for them but

could not find them, so I got replacements. One
the day I that the keys came up missing, Thierry
was there and he approached me, and I said what
are you doing here. He said to get the keys; if you
don't want the money I'll take it with my friend. I
said how did you know I would be here,
he said I took your work schedule from your truck
when I met you. I yelled at him and told him to get
away from me. He said well you can be mad or
you can get paid! I am going to get those keys
with or without you. I said its without me! I went
to work on the roof after getting the keys from
you. And while I was up there I stated to think of
how much I could use the money to expand my
business and take care of my baby on the way. I
thought of how easy it would be to distract you
and open the safe. So I decided that I would join
Thierry and take the money but not that night
because it was not planned out and I did not want to
go back to prison. After the work was done, Thierry
was still there with his friend that worked there. So I
pulled him to the side and told him I have the keys,
but we are going to do this my way, so give me your
name and number and I'll call you to talk about this
more, and we are not going to include your friend.
He said ok, gave me his info. and I left.
After thinking about it for a couple of days, I
approached my wife saying I think I've found a easy
way to make a lot of money. I explained to her about
Thierry, and all that he told me about the

keys. She told me I was not going to do it! I said I think I am and I already have the keys, and we are not going to use weapons, no one will get hurt I promise. She said that if you are going to do this then I am going with you. I said no way, you have our baby, and so you cannot be there! She said she wanted to make sure that I was all right and that she would worry. I said well we may need a get away driver, so I'll let you know.

I contacted Thierry, and told him it's was a go. He said I have a gun just in case. I said no! No weapons will be used, because I will distract the manager while you open the safe. He said ok. So we planned on doing the robbery the next time I serviced the place. Well on September 24th, I went to the Ernst Steam Cleaning office to pick up my check, it was short, and I needed money right away. So I called Thierry and told him it was going to take place tonight, but we would need another way in because I was not scheduled to service that place for a couple of weeks. Thierry came by my house around 12:30 am and I explained to him why things had to change. He understood, as he knew that he needed me to pull it off.

So Thierry, me and my wife got in my truck and started to drive to McDonalds, and on the way we stopped to get some gas. We continued on, and once at the scene we parked and waited until all the employees left except for you. We had decided that if someone stayed with you the whole time we would not do it, because we did not plan for two

people or more. We were parked at the back of the parking lot in front, facing the store so we could watch everything. If you remember not long after they left is when he came to the door. He was disguised. He had on the same clothes that as I had on. (Black shirt, black jeans, and Reebok tennis shoes.) At this time we parked right outside the front door at the far curb. It was my red and white truck. My wife was now in the drivers seat and kept the engine running to make a quick getaway.
His goal was to keep you confused so that it would make it hard for anyone to I.D. us. So he approached the front door, knock and said that he had the keys that were missing. After you both talked and he gave you his name and said that he came for compensation and then pulled the screw driver out. (I say it was a screw driver cause this is what he told us after the fact.)

As you ran and he ran after you I ran in behind him and he hid behind the counter while I stopped you at the office door. I made you go to the safe and open it up. I told you not to look at me and when you put your head down I stood up and Thierry took over. I was now behind the counter as he made you crawl on your hands and knees to the office. He was crawling behind you. I want you to know that this was done to prevent people from seeing you or him. This is why we also kept hiding in front of the counter. I went to the car with the money and gave it to my wife. I tried to come back in but the door was locked. I could not see inside the office because the door was closed. I was knocking on the door, trying to get Thierry to let me in. I was afraid of what he was doing because he was only supposed to take you to the office and tell you to wait 30 minutes before leaving. My wife was hollering, "What is he doing, why is he taking so long!" I said, "I don't know." I banged on the door harder, you probably did not hear because of the trauma you were suffering. I started to think the worst because; I knew how bad he wanted to bring a weapon. He later said that he found the knife on the counter but now I believe he brought it with him. This was my fault cause I never should have taken him up on his proposition and this might not have happened. Finally, he came out, and I said, "what took you so long." He said I just had to talk to her to make sure she didn't talk. We got in the truck and my wife drove off. I smelled a metallic odor, and I said "What is that smell? It smells like blood!" He said, "Well it might be hers." I said "What! Did you kill her!" He said "No, but I stabbed her and cut her throat, but not enough to kill her she will live." My wife started to cry. I was furious, so I elbowed him hard, and we started to fight in the truck. My wife pulled over and I opened the door and dragged him outside. I got on top of him and pinned him to the ground and said,

"WHY, WHY ! We agreed no one would get
hurt." He said, "it was just to make sure she didn't
talk." My wife said,
"We have to go back and help her."
But we all then agree that the police would
probably be there by now. Thierry said 'that if we
tell that he was involved he would make sure that
we went down with him. He knew that my wife
was pregnant and reminded us that our child
would be without both its parents. We got back in
the truck and counted the money, it was only just
over $400.00. I said, "that's not what you said it
would be." He said, "I was hoping to get into the
drop-safe, I know there is thousands in there.
However, she said the morning manager that open
the store has the other key. So it takes two
people to open the safe." I said, "so you tried to
kill this lady over money!" He said,
"I did not try to kill her she will live, and it was
not over money it was about her identifying us."
I said;
"she cant **ID** me!"
My wife said,,
"Roger, just let him have the money, drop him off
and lets forget about this it was a bad idea
anyway."
So we dropped Thierry off and we went home. We
couldn't sleep and we went to check on you. But
the police were there, so we knew that you had
been helped. Then when we got home, we called

the hospital to see how you were doing. And they said you were in serious but stable condition. We worried all day, and prayed that you would survive. We are so sorry again that we did this horrible thing to you and your family. We can never change what we did. We can just promise that we will never do it again. I know that there is some gaps in your memory and this is understandable, seeming that you suffered such a traumatic event. And I wanted you to finally have the truth, the whole truth, and nothing but the truth. So that you may finally begin to get closure if that is even possible. I will understand if you never forgive me, and you never support my parole, as this is your choice. But I am repentant and very sorry for what I have done. Whatever you need to make things better I will try to aide in that process if you will allow me to. May God Bless you and your Family and may you have peace all the days of your life!

Sincerely yours,

Roger Jason Lee

(As the reader, you now have more information and fact manipulation to make a decision as to guilt or innocence. Was it Mr. Lee or Mr. Thierry? Or was it both? Or did Mr. Lee conjure up everything about Mr. Thierry except for the officials who responded to the Thierry involvement or who did not respond. Can you believe him when he says that he did not reveal everything that occurred because of a pregnant wife and later a daughter who had to turn 18 before he would admit to guilt in a robbery but not in an attempt to hurt the victim?)

Guilty ☐

Innocent ☐

Thanks for reading, "The Writ". Now you can choose your Verdict:

www.ingramcontent.com/pod-product-compliance
Lightning Source LLC
Chambersburg PA
CBHW060248290526
45789CB00001B/243